THE HANDBOOK OF

BRITISH RAILWAYS

C000227080

STEAM MOTIVE POWER DEPOTS

CONTENTS

VOLUME TWO
CENTRAL ENGLAND
EAST ANGLIA & WALES
PAUL SMITH

PLATFORM 5

Dedicated to the memory of my Father-in-Law

ARTHUR

who sadly passed away before this volume was completed.

The demise of steam is epitomised in this view of ex-GWR 5700 Class 0–6–0PT No. 4696, devoid of all "bolt on goodies" it typified the demeanour of the steam locomotive in its last days. This view was taken on March 15th, 1967 at **TYSELEY MPD** some five months after closure and a week after steam had been officially banished from the West Midlands. *John Edgington*

ACKNOWLEDGEMENTS

One of the most gratifying aspects of compiling a work such as this is the people that are met, the contacts made by correspondence or just voices on the end of a 'phone, all offering information or advice in a cheerful ungrudging manner. May I offer my thanks to them all and particularly so to:

Alan Peters, HN James, Maurice Newman, Chris Bush, Roy Peters, Nick Pigott, Chris Bates (BBC Pebble Mill Press Officer) and Philip Stuart.
WT (Bill) Stubbs for again chipping in with the bulk of the photographs.
Alec Swain, Ken Fairey, Bill Potter, Bernard Matthews, John Edgington and Allan Sommerfield for access to their photographic collections.
Mr R. Fairclough, Tony Rawlings, Karen Amies and Ruth Long at the Cambridge University Map Library. No praise could be high enough to describe the whole hearted assistance and co-operation afforded to me, both by post and during the visits to the library. Their cheerful demeanour turned what could have been a long weary task into a pleasure.
Bob Hadley for checking the copy and final proof reading.

Finally many thanks to the *"better half"* Shirley for putting up with the constant clutter of artwork, paper, magazines, notes and books that litter every nook and cranny of the house. Her encouragement and participation in trudging around shed sites all over the country has been greatly appreciated.

Artwork and Design by Paul Smith.
All shed maps are reproduced from various Ordnance Survey Maps with permission of the Controller of Her Majesty's Stationery Office, ©Crown Copyright.
All shed maps are reproduced by permission of The Syndics of Cambridge University Library.

Published by Platform 5 Publishing Ltd., Lydgate House, Lydgate Lane, Sheffield S10 5FH, England.
Printed by Amadeus Press, 517 Leeds Road, Huddersfield, West Yorkshire, HD2 1YJ. Cover by Maxwell Data Management, Slack Lane, Derby.
ISBN 0 906579 95 3

THE
HANDBOOK
OF

BRITISH RAILWAYS

STEAM MOTIVE POWER DEPOTS

PREFACE TO VOLUME 2

This volume continues the series using the same format, although with minor typographical alterations. The number of pages has been increased from 96 to 112 and not only reflects the larger number of depots contained in Parts 5 to 9, but also allows a small increase in photographic content. However, as in *Volume 1* pressure of space precludes the inclusion of photographs of all the sheds.

The area covered in this volume contains many contrasts, from some of the most remote and sparsely populated regions south of the border, with railway systems to match, to one of the world's largest concentrations of branch lines, mineral lines and steam locomotives - The Welsh Valleys. Many of the small sheds were in a great variety of designs and even the GWR with its mind-numbing attempt to standardise all that it touched managed to possess, and bestow to BR, some extremely non-standard buildings.

The Central Midlands, encompassing Birmingham, Coventry and Northampton in effect formed the southern edge of the industrial heartland of England and the railway system, although nowhere as near as concentrated as in the North Midlands and Lancashire and Yorkshire (See *Volume 3*) reflected the importance of the region.

East Anglia, with its large number of little-used lines and, beyond the borders of London commuterland, small concentration of locomotives was a prime candidate for early dieselisation and much of it succumbed before the 1960s.

Beeching soon put paid to many of the branch lines that proliferated in Wales and East Anglia, and with it most of the steam sheds became (for some) just fond memories. The cross country lines that fed into these extremities closed at the same time and the railway systems that they serviced basically withered away. It always seems ironic that in these days of fast road travel anyone contemplating to drive a motor vehicle from Central Wales across to East Anglia rarely glimpses a motorway, let alone is able to use one and is faced with an unremitting slog of single carriage roadways, little changed from the days when railways were a more than viable alternative. Such is progress and merely illustrates the apparent preoccupation with all roads leading to London and hang the rest.

BRITISH RAILWAYS

PAUL SMITH
Birmingham 1989

CROMER BEACH *(Sid Nash)*

ERRATUM FOR VOLUME I

From correspondence received so far *Volume I* appears to have escaped fairly lightly from gremlins and suchlike. However one major *faux pas* undoubtedly occurred on Page 21 where, as Sid Nash points out, Battle of Britain Class 4–6–2 No. 34090 was described as *66 SQUADRON* rather than *SIR EUSTACE MISSENDEN, SOUTHERN RAILWAY*, its correct name.

A less dramatic error can be found on Page 8 where, amongst the shed codes, Penicuik (Sub of 64A) inadvertently acquired an additional 'c'.

Demolition dates would appear to be as contentious, if not more so, than those appertaining to closures. Philip Stuart took me to task on several sites and suggested that the dates given were a bit off beam. From a practical point of view demolitions are perceived purely from observations (as compared to closures which in many instances are given "official" dates) and only by being in the right place at the right time can the precise demolition date be ascertained.

As a result these are usually estimated at some point between the last time the depot was reported as standing and the first time reported as demolished. It would be very difficult indeed for one person alone to be able to record demolitions from his own personal observations, and hence there is a strong reliance upon reports from others. Readers may rest assured that as errors are notified and more information is garnered an updated Site Usage and Demolition Date for each shed, wherever possible, shall appear in the Index and Bibliography in *Volume 4* when it is published in 1990.

BIBLIOGRAPHY

The principal sources of reference for this volume were:
An Historical Survey of Great Western Engine Sheds 1947 by E.Lyons (OPC) SBN 902888 16 1
An Historical Survey of Great Western Engine Sheds 1837–1947 by E.Lyons and E.Mountford (OPC) ISBN 0 86093 019 X

LMS Engine Sheds Vols I (ISBN 0 906867 02 9), 2 (ISBN 0 906867 05 3) and 4 (ISBN 0 906867 20 7) by Chris Hawkins & George Reeve (Wild Swan Publications)
Great Eastern Railway Engine Sheds Parts 1 (ISBN 0 906867 40 1) and 2 (ISBN 0 906867 48 7) by Chris Hawkins and George Reeve (Wild Swan Publications)
The British Locomotive Shed Directory (1947) by Aidan L.F. Fuller
British Railways Pre-Grouping Atlas and Gazetteer by W.P.Conolly (Railway Publications Ltd)
Complete British Railways Maps and Gazetteer 1825–1985 by C.J.Wignall (OPC)
BR Steam Motive Power Depots ER (ISBN 0 7110 1193 1) and LMR (ISBN 0 7110 1019 6) by Paul Bolger (Ian Allan)

CARDIFF EAST DOCK *(John Edgington)*

PENMAENPOOL *(Alec Swain)*

THE SHEDS
LISTED BY GEOGRAPHICAL AREA

The country has been divided into 19 Parts and each Part is further sub-divided into Counties and Large Conurbations. These Parts and Sub-Divisions are purely a convenience, based on pre-war County administrations and having no pretensions as to pinpointing towns and villages within "modern" boundaries. BR Regions have been acknowledged, as with regards to the coding of a depot, but each area has been considered as an autonomous unit within which all sheds are dealt with, regardless of origin or operating region. This is designed to present the reader with a complete, concise, rather than fragmented, record of the existence of BR Steam Motive Power Depots within an area.

Each PART is prefaced with a map showing the area covered, indicating all the railway lines built within its boundaries (but not necessarily passing into BR ownership nor, indeed, still extant in 1948) and an index of all the sheds dealt with in that part. Each COUNTY or CONURBATION is prefaced with another map, this time showing the approximate location of each depot relative to the railway network.

Within each sub-division, each FACILITY is identified by name and regional code and LOCATED with reference to nearby stations and lines and pinpointed within about 100 metres by an OS reference. The DIRECTIONS, in the style of Aidan Fullers famous shed directories, are contemporary to its existence. Of all contentious issues with regard to engine sheds, none is more fraught with pot holes than the CLOSURE DATE. Many of those listed are the 'official' ones, but this is by no means decisive. As far as operational requirements went it could have meant an end of a permanent locomotive allocation or permanent staffing, neither of which would have precluded further use of the depot. Indeed, actually closing the building may have just meant that locomotives were serviced and stabled in the yard. Many of the servicing facilities just dwindled away, there being no, nor needing any, "official" date. Hence the OUT OF USE, in many cases no more than just an intelligent stab in the dark.

The DESCRIPTION is of a brief nature, the abbreviation "TS" being shorthand for track straighthouse. The POST CLOSURE HISTORY traces the use of the buildings and site following closure to steam.

Each of the depots is indicated on a reproduction of an ORDNANCE SURVEY MAP, most of these maps are at a scale of 1:5000 and dated as near as possible to 1948. The object is to present a permanent record of the location within a large area, so that although the shed may have long gone the site can be located by reference to other features, roads or buildings. Although the intention of these maps is not to specifically provide accurate track diagrams many do, indeed, provide this information. Where diagrams are of a more recent vintage the depot has been superimposed over its original site, in many instances providing a very interesting contrast. Further commentary, clarifying the location of the site within an area, the adjacency of the local road network, and other points of interest has been added.

Finally, many of the depots have been illustrated by means of a PHOTOGRAPH.

An INDEX, at the end of this volume lists the sheds in alphabetical order and gives a page reference. A complete Index and Bibliography Section for the whole series can be found at the back of *Volume 4.*

A fully coded list of British Railways Motive Power Depots, based upon the first one published in 1950, appears in Volume 1 of this series.

PART FIVE

EAST ANGLIA

ESSEX   NORFOLK   SUFFOLK   CAMBRIDGESHIRE

BRITISH RAILWAYS

ESSEX

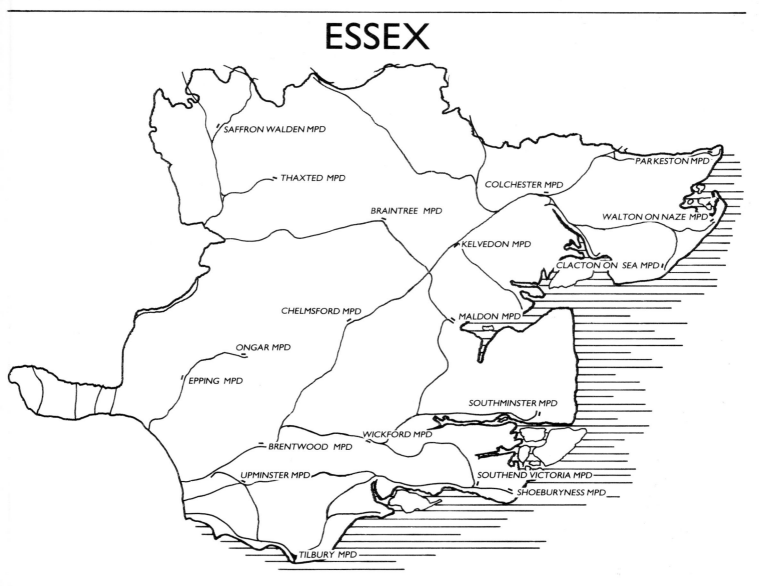

SAFFRON WALDEN MPD

THAXTED MPD

PARKESTON MPD

COLCHESTER MPD

BRAINTREE MPD

WALTON ON NAZE MPD

KELVEDON MPD

CLACTON ON SEA MPD

CHELMSFORD MPD

MALDON MPD

ONGAR MPD

EPPING MPD

SOUTHMINSTER MPD

WICKFORD MPD

BRENTWOOD MPD

UPMINSTER MPD

SOUTHEND VICTORIA MPD

SHOEBURYNESS MPD

TILBURY MPD

30A(s) ONGAR

Location: On the west side of Ongar Station. (OS Map Ref;TL550035)
Directions: Entrance to the shed is effected from the station platform.
Closed: September 25th, 1949
Description: Originally a brick built ITS through road shed but by BR days consisting of an engine pit and track only. There are no shed buildings.
Post Closure History: *Yard used as a Stabling Point until 1957. Lines lifted.*

A pre-war view of the shed building at **ONGAR MPD**, by BR days the structure had disappeared and locomotives were serviced over the remaining engine pit.
Bernard Matthews Collection

CHIPPING ONGAR

N△   0 FEET   500   © CROWN COPYRIGHT

Map Dated: 1970
Site Location: In Chipping Ongar town centre, on the west side of High Street (A113)
Track Status: Ongar Station and line are operational.

30A(s) CHELMSFORD

Location: Sited in a small Goods Yard situated north of the line, east of Chelmsford Station. (OS Map Ref:TL713075)

Directions: Turn left outside of the station along the approach road and left again along Duke Street. Almost immediately turn left into Victoria Road, bear right and turn left along New Street. Proceed under the railway bridge and turn right into the Goods Yard. The shed is at the end of this yard.

Out of Use: 1960

Description: Consisting solely of an Engine Pit and Water Column.

Post Closure History: Tracks still in situ, although the pit is filled in, and the Mess Room is still standing.(1988)

Ex-LNER Class N7 0–6–2T locomotives Nos. 69727 and 69699 standing over the engine pit at **CHELMSFORD MPD** on July 12th, 1958. *Ken Fairey*

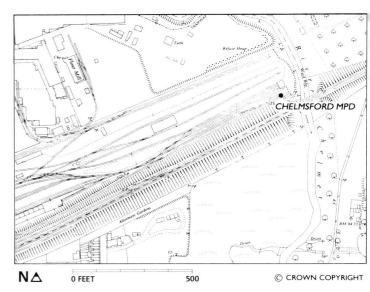

Map Dated: 1951

Site Location: East of the town centre, on the west bank of the River Chelmer.

Track Status: Chelmsford Station and line are operational.

30A(s) BRENTWOOD

Location: On the north side of Brentwood Station. (OS Map Ref: TQ594930)

Directions: Entrance to the shed is effected from the station platform.

Out of Use: 1949

Description: A brick and wooden built 3TS dead ended shed.

Post Closure History: Demolished. The shed yard was used as a Stabling Point for a Petrol Shunter until September 1956.

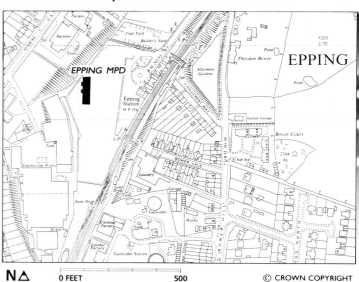

Map Dated: 1950

Site Location: In the south of the town, on the east side of Warley Hill (B186)

Track Status: Brentwood & Warley Station and line are intact.

30A(s) EPPING

Location: In the Goods Yard at the west side of Epping Station. (OS Map Ref: TL461015)

Directions: Entrance to the Goods Yard is effected from the Station Approach Road, opposite the entrance to the Station.

Closed: November 18th, 1957.

Description: A brick built 2TS dead ended shed.

Post Closure History: Demolished. Now site of Car Park

Map Dated: 1970 (Shed Superimposed)

Site Location: South of the town centre, on the west side of High Road (B1393).

Track Status: Epping (LT) Station and line are operational.

30D(s) SOUTHMINSTER

Location: On the east side of Southminster Station. (OS Map Ref: TQ962995)
Directions: Entrance to the shed is effected from the station platform.
Out of Use: September 1956.
Description: Formerly a brick built 2TS through road shed it was roofless by BR days and only the turning and watering facilities were used.
Post Closure History: *Demolished*

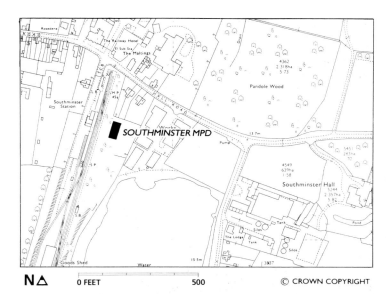

SOUTHMINSTER MPD only offered basic servicing facilities to visiting locomotives by BR days. The roofless structure was photographed on February 5th, 1955.
John Edgington

Map Dated: 1973 (Shed Superimposed)
Site Location: South east of the town centre, on the east side of the B1021
Track Status: Southminster Station and line are operational.

30D(s) WICKFORD

Location: West of the line, at the north end of Wickford Station. (OS Map Ref: TQ745937)
Directions: Entrance to the shed is effected from the station platform.
Out of Use: November 1954.
Description: Consisting of an Engine Pit, Turntable, Coaling and Watering Facilities only. There are no shed buildings.
Post Closure History: *Lines lifted.*

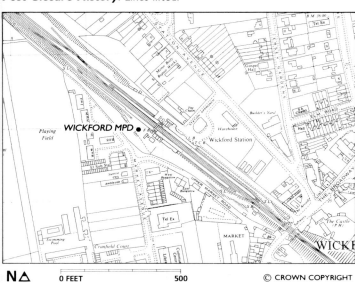

Map Dated: 1969
Site Location: North west of the town centre, on the west side of The Broadway (A132)
Track Status: Wickford Station and line are operational.

30E(s) WALTON ON NAZE

Location: On the north side of Walton on Naze Station. (OS Map Ref: TM251214)
Directions: Entrance to the shed is effected from the station platform.
Closed: June 17th, 1963
Description: A brick built 1TS dead ended shed.
Post Closure History: *Demolished*

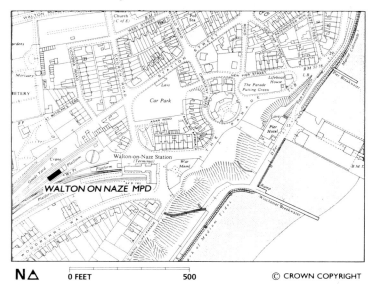

Map Dated: 1957
Site Location: In the town centre, south of Walton Road (B1336)
Track Status: Walton on Naze Station and line are operational

30E(s) BRAINTREE

Location: Situated in the Goods Yard, on the north side of Braintree Station. (OS Map Ref: TL764228)

Directions: Turn right outside of the station along Approach Road, bear right and proceed along Railway Street. The entrance to the Goods Yard is on the right hand side, and the shed is at the far end of this yard.

Closed: November 1959

Description: A brick built 1TS through road shed.

Post Closure History: Demolished.

BRAINTREE MPD on April 16th, 1949   *John Edgington*

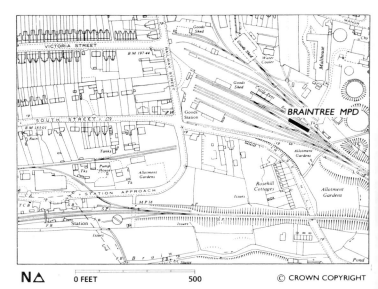

Map Dated: 1953

Site Location: South of the town centre, south of Coggeshall Road (A120)

Track Status: Braintree Station and line (east of the station) are operational.

30E(s) CLACTON ON SEA

Location: North of Clacton on Sea Station, west of the line. (OS Map Ref: TM179159)

Directions: A pathway leads to the shed from the end of the station platform.

Closed: April 13th, 1959 (Steam). June 17th, 1963 (Totally)

Description: A wooden built 2TS dead ended shed.

Post Closure History: Demolished. After closure to steam, the shed was extended to accomodate emu's.

CLACTON ON SEA MPD on September 2nd, 1960. By this time the original steam shed had been extended to accomodate the longer length of emu sets. The difference between the two buildings is plainly obvious in this view.

WT Stubbs Collection

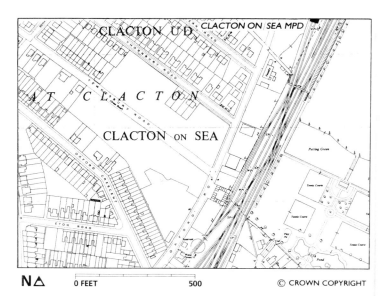

Map Dated: 1953

Site Location: In the east of the town, on the south side of Oxford Road

Track Status: Clacton on Sea Station and line are operational.

30E(s) KELVEDON

Location: North of the line, at the west end of Kelvedon Low Level Station. (OS Map Ref: TL864194)

Directions: Entrance to the shed is effected from the station platform.

Closed: May 5th, 1951.

Description: A concrete and corrugated iron 1TS dead ended shed.

Post Closure History: Demolished. Floors traceable. Site Unused. (1984)

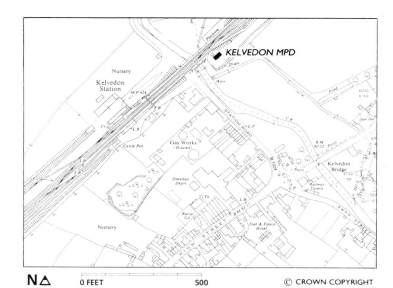

NΔ   0 FEET   500   © CROWN COPYRIGHT

Map Dated: 1954 (Shed Superimposed)

Site Location: In the north of the town, on the north side of High Street (A12)

Track Status: Kelvedon Low Level Station closed in 1951. Lines lifted. Kelvedon Station and line are operational.

A pre-war view of the small shed building at **KELVEDON MPD**

Allan Sommerfield Collection

30E(s) MALDON

Location: East of the line, at the south end of Maldon East & Heybridge Station. (OS Map Ref: TL855074)

Directions: Entrance to the shed is effected from the station platform.

Out of Use: 1960.

Description: A brick built 2TS dead ended shed.

Post Closure History: Still Standing (1989)

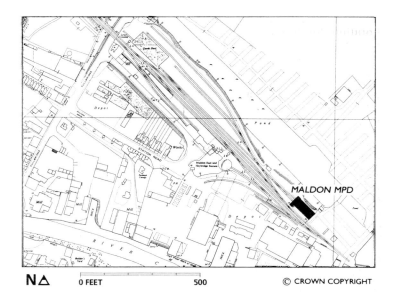

NΔ   0 FEET   500   © CROWN COPYRIGHT

Map Dated: 1959

Site Location: North of the town centre, on the north bank of the River Chelmer.

Track Status: Maldon East & Heybridge Station closed in 1964. Lines lifted.

The unusual style of architecture is clearly visible in this pre-war view of **MALDON MPD**.

Allan Sommerfield Collection

30E COLCHESTER

Location: On the north side of the line, east of Colchester Station. (OS Map Ref: TL995263)

Directions: Turn right outside the north side of the station, along the approach road. The shed entrance is in North Station Road opposite the end of this road.

Closed: November 2nd, 1959.

Description: A brick built 3TS shed with 1 through road.

Post Closure History: Demolished. The site is now a Car Park. (1989)

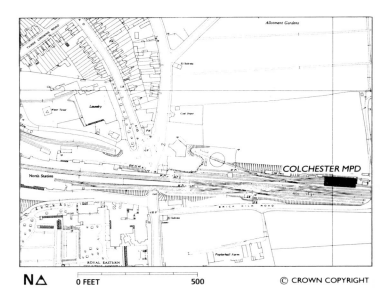

Map Dated: 1952

Site Location: In the north of the town on the east side of the A134.

Track Status: Colchester Station and line are operational.

The spectre of electrification hangs heavily over **COLCHESTER MPD** barely six weeks away from closure when photographed on September 13th, 1959. *Ken Fairey*

30F PARKESTON

Location: North of the line at the east end of Harwich Parkeston Quay Station. (OS Map Ref: TM242325)

Directions: A path runs from the station platform to the shed.

Closed: January 2nd, 1961.

Description: A brick built 4TS dead ended shed.

Post Closure History: Demolished. Now site of Freightliner Terminal.

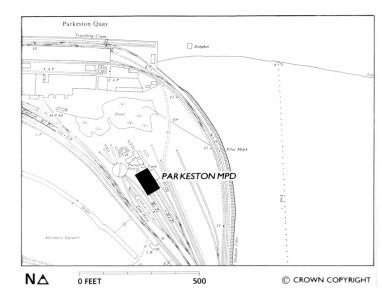

Map Dated: 1955

Site Location: About 1 mile west of Harwich, north of the A604.

Track Status: Parkeston Quay Station and line are operational.

British Railways was much in its infancy judging by the mixture of legends applied to the sides of the locomotives. **PARKESTON QUAY MPD** was photographed on April 17th, 1949.
John Edgington

31A(s) SAFFRON WALDEN

Location: South of the line, east of Saffron Walden Station. (OS Map Ref: TL542387)

Directions: Turn right outside of the station, right across the bridge and left down Farmadine Grove running parallel to the line. A gate in the fence on the left hand side leads to the shed.

Out of Use: July 1958

Description: A brick built 1TS through road shed.

Post Closure History: *Remained intact until 1964. Now demolished. Site Unused. (1976)*

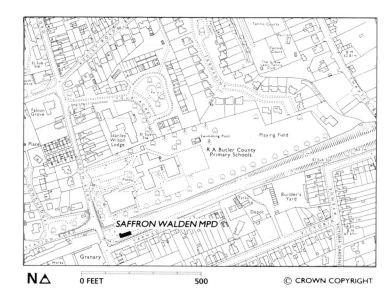

Map Dated: 1970
Site Location: South of the town centre, west of Thaxted Road (B184)
Track Status: Saffron Walden Station closed in 1964. Lines lifted

An interesting post-steam view of **SAFFRON WALDEN MPD**, with a diesel shunter tucked inside the shed building and a diesel railbus calling at the station. Photographed on September 3rd, 1960. *WT Stubbs Collection*

31A(S) THAXTED

Location: At the end of the line, at the east end of Thaxted Station. (OS Map Ref: TL605301)

Directions: Entrance to the shed is effected from the station platform.

Closed: September 15th, 1952.

Description: A brick built 1TS dead ended shed.

Post Closure History: *Still standing. In use as a Garage. (1980)*

Ex-LNER Class J69 0–6–0T No. 68579 takes a breather between duties outside of **THAXTED MPD** on September 10th, 1952. *Sid Nash*

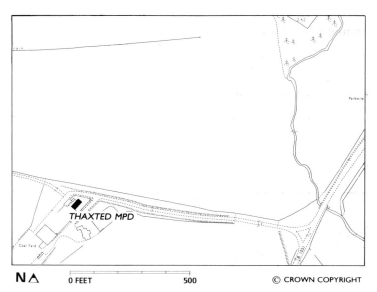

Map Dated: 1977
Site Location: About 1 mile south west of the town, adjacent to the north side of the B1051
Track Status: Thaxted Station closed in 1952. Line lifted.

33A(s) UPMINSTER

Location: North of the line, east of Upminster Station. (OS Map Ref: TQ564869)

Directions: Entrance to the shed is effected from the station platform.

Closed: September 17th, 1956.

Description: A brick built 1TS through road shed, latterly roofless.

Post Closure History: Demolished. Site now occupied by sidings. (1989)

UPMINSTER MPD stands in the background as ex-LMS Class 1 0–4–4T No. 58089 receives attention before taking out the Grays branch train. This view was taken on July 11th, 1953.   *Allan Sommerfield Collection*

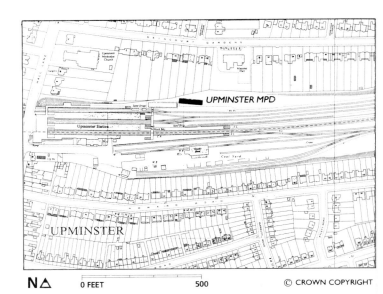

N△   0 FEET   500   © CROWN COPYRIGHT

Map Dated: 1965

Site Location: In the centre of the town, on the north side of St.Mary's Lane (B187).

Track Status: Upminster Station and line are operational.

33B TILBURY

Location: In the triangle of the Tilbury Riverside to Tilbury Town to Low Street lines. (OS Map Ref: TQ644758)

Directions: Leave Tilbury Riverside Station by the western exit, proceed along, parallel to the railway line, and continue into Ferry Road. A footbridge leads to the shed from the right hand side of this road.

Closed: June 1962.

Description: A dilapidated corrugated iron 4TS through road shed.

Post Closure History: Demolished

The corrugated iron shed at **TILBURY MPD** always looked a cold, windy place to work in. Two BR standard locomotives of varying vintage simmer in the shed yard on April 20th, 1961.   *Ken Fairey*

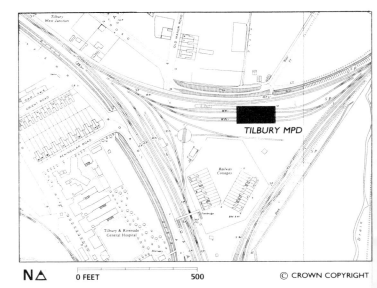

N△   0 FEET   500   © CROWN COPYRIGHT

Map Dated: 1960

Site Location: In the south of the town, adjacent to the north side of Ferry Road.

Track Status: Tilbury Station and line are operational.

33C SHOEBURYNESS

Location; The shed is on the north side of Shoeburyness Station. (OS Map Ref: TQ940851)

Directions; Entrance to the shed is effected from the station platform.

Closed; June 18th, 1962

Description; A brick built 2TS dead ended shed with a smaller and lightweight 2TS dead ended shed built alongside.

Post Closure History; Demolished. Site of Industrial Estate.

Ex-LMS and BR 2–6–4T engines were very much the bread and butter of **SHOEBURYNESS MPD** as this general view of the shed and yard, taken on March 17th, 1962, reveals.   *Alec Swain*

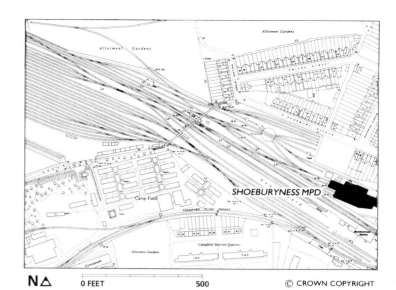

N△   0 FEET   500   © CROWN COPYRIGHT

Map Dated: 1962
Site Location: In the centre of the town.
Track Status: Shoeburyness Station and line are operational.

30D SOUTHEND VICTORIA

Location: East of the line, north of Southend Victoria Station. (OS Map Ref: TQ881864)

Directions: Turn left outside of the station, left into an alleyway and this leads to the shed.

Out of Use: 1957.

Description: A brick built 2TS through road shed.

Post Closure History: Demolished

A trio of ex-LTS 4–4–2T engines Nos. 41975, 41976 & 41949 occupying the shed yard at **SOUTHEND ON SEA MPD** on February 5th, 1955.   *John Edgington*

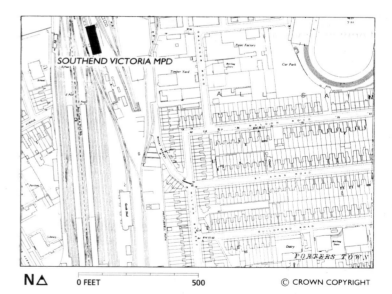

N△   0 FEET   500   © CROWN COPYRIGHT

Map Dated: 1951
Site Location: On the east side of Victoria Avenue (A127) in the centre of the town.
Track Status: Southend Victoria Station and line are operational.

NORFOLK

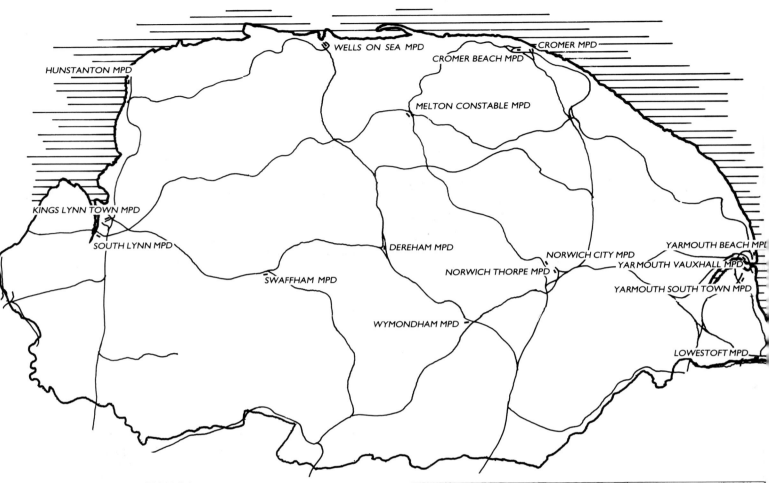

HUNSTANTON MPD

WELLS ON SEA MPD

CROMER MPD

CROMER BEACH MPD

MELTON CONSTABLE MPD

KINGS LYNN TOWN MPD

SOUTH LYNN MPD

DEREHAM MPD

NORWICH CITY MPD

YARMOUTH BEACH MPD

NORWICH THORPE MPD

YARMOUTH VAUXHALL MPD

SWAFFHAM MPD

YARMOUTH SOUTH TOWN MPD

WYMONDHAM MPD

LOWESTOFT MPD

31C KINGS LYNN TOWN

Location: North of the line, at the east end of Kings Lynn Station. (OS Map Ref: TF626205)
Directions: A path leads from the north side of the station to the shed.
Closed: April 12th, 1959
Description: A brick built 4TS through road shed.
Post Closure History: Demolished. Now site of sidings. (1980)

KINGS LYNN MPD parades some of its collection of ex-GE locomotives on a sunny October day in 1953.
Allan Sommerfield Collection

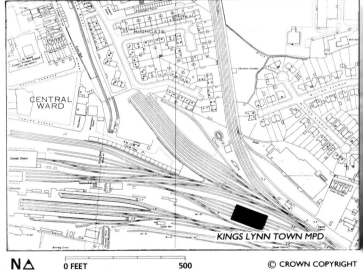

N△   0 FEET   500   © CROWN COPYRIGHT

KINGS LYNN TOWN MPD

Map Dated: 1967 (Shed Superimposed)
Site Location: East of the town centre on the east side of Blackfriars Road (B1154)
Track Status: Kings Lynn Station and line are operational.

31C(s) HUNSTANTON

Location: West of the line, south of Hunstanton Station. (OS Map Ref: TF671405)

Directions: Entrance to the shed is effected from the station platform.

Closed: November 1958.

Description: A brick built 2TS dead ended shed.

Post Closure History: Demolished

A general view of **HUNSTANTON MPD** taken from the footbridge on August 29th, 1960. *WT Stubbs Collection*

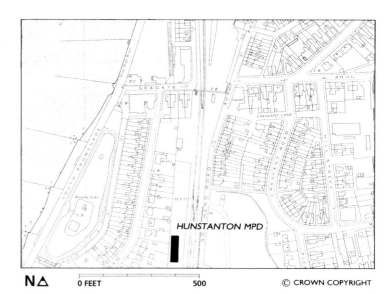

HUNSTANTON MPD

N△   0 FEET   500   © CROWN COPYRIGHT

Map Dated: 1970 (Shed Superimposed)

Site Location: On the west side of the town.

Track Status: Hunstanton Station closed in 1969. Lines lifted.

31D SOUTH LYNN

Location: South of the line, at the east end of South Lynn Station. (OS Map Ref: TF618179)

Directions: Turn left outside of Kings Lynn Station into Blackfriars Road, left into St.James Road, proceed along London Road, turn right into Wisbech Road and fork left into Saddlebow Road. The shed entrance is a gate on the left hand side about half a mile along just past the railway bridge.

Closed: February 1959.

Description: Originally a wooden built 4TS dead ended shed it was rebuilt in asbestos sheeting shortly before closure.

Post Closure History: Used as a NCL depot for some years, it remained derelict until demolition in 1989.

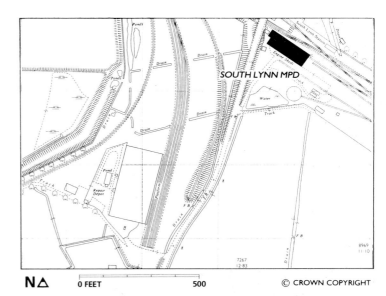

SOUTH LYNN MPD

N△   0 FEET   500   © CROWN COPYRIGHT

Map Dated: 1966

Site Location: About 1 mile south of Kings Lynn, south of the A47.

Track Status: All lines lifted.

SOUTH LYNN MPD on May 4th, 1952. This view shows the ex-M&GN shed in its original form as inherited by BR. The depot earned universal fame in 1959 when it was rebuilt and then closed in the same year. *John Edgington*

32A NORWICH THORPE

Location: South of the line, east of Norwich Thorpe Station. (OS Map Ref: TG241081)

Directions: Leave the station and enter Lower Clarence Road. Proceed along this road, turn right into Clarence Road and the shed entrance is on the right hand side, just past the bridge.

Closed: April 2nd, 1962 (Steam)

Description: A brick built 4TS through road shed.

Post Closure History: *Still Standing. In use as a Diesel Depot (Code NR) until 1985.*

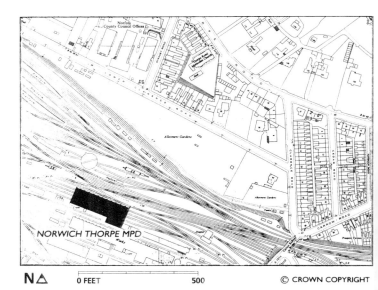

N△   0 FEET   500   © CROWN COPYRIGHT

Map Dated: 1958

Site Location: In the south east of the city, west of Carrow Road (A1074)

Track Status: Norwich Thorpe Station and line are operational.

A totally dieselised **NORWICH THORPE MPD** with Class 31, 37 and 47 locomotives dominating the shed yard.   *WT Stubbs Collection*

32G(s) NORWICH CITY

Location: East of the line, north of Norwich City Station. (OS Map Ref: TG225095)

Directions: A boarded crossing leads from the station platforms to the shed.

Closed: February 28th, 1959.

Description: A corrugated iron 2TS dead ended shed.

Post Closure History: *Shed building removed.*

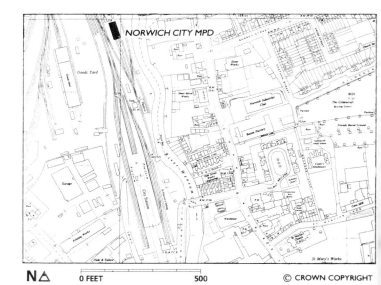

N△   0 FEET   500   © CROWN COPYRIGHT

Map Dated: 1956

Site Location: North of the city centre, on the west bank of the River Wensum.

Track Status: Norwich City Station closed in 1959. Lines lifted.

The shed building was dismantled and re-erected at Weybourne on the North Norfolk Railway.

Two ex-LMS moguls manoeuvre in the shed yard at **NORWICH CITY MPD** on February 28th, 1959.   *Sid Nash*

32A(s) CROMER

Location: East of the line, adjacent to Cromer (High) Station. (OS Map Ref: TG224410)

Directions: Entrance to the shed is effected from the station platform.

Closed: September 1954.

Description: A brick built ITS dead ended shed.

Post Closure History: Demolished shortly after closure. The site remained unused until 1987 when it became a housing estate. (1988)

An indistinct, but nonetheless interesting pre-war view of **CROMER MPD**
Allan Sommerfield Collection

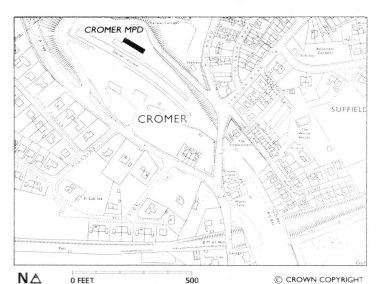

N△   0 FEET   500   © CROWN COPYRIGHT

Map Dated: 1970 (Shed Superimposed)

Site Location: In the town centre, on the north side of Norwich Road (A149)

Track Status: Cromer (High) Station closed in 1954. Lines lifted.

32G(s) CROMER BEACH

Location: On the north side of Cromer Beach Station. (OS Map Ref: TG214421)

Directions: Entrance to the shed is effected from the station platform.

Out of Use: 1959

Description: A brick built ITS dead ended shed

Post Closure History: Still Standing (1987)

Ex-LNER Classes B12/3 4–6–0 No. 61540 and B17 4–6–0 No. 61656 share the accomodation at **CROMER BEACH MPD** on September 19th, 1954.
John Edgington

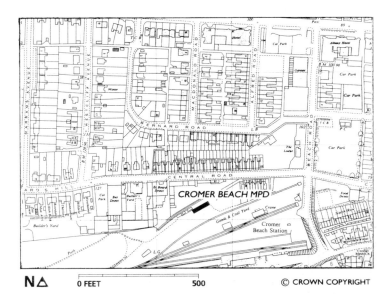

N△   0 FEET   500   © CROWN COPYRIGHT

Map Dated: 1970

Site Location: West of the town centre, on the west side of Beach Road.

Track Status: Cromer (Beach) Station and line are operational.

32A(s) DEREHAM

Location: In the triangle of lines formed by the Dereham–Kings Lynn–Norwich routes, south of Dereham Station. (OS Map Ref: TF994129)
Directions: Entrance to the shed is effected from the station platform.
Closed: September 19th, 1955 (Steam).
Description: A brick built 2TS dead ended shed.
Post Closure History: Used for servicing dmus but now demolished. Site Unused

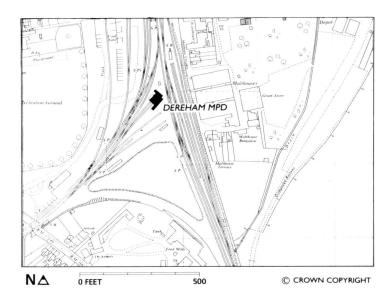

N△   0 FEET   500   © CROWN COPYRIGHT

Map Dated: 1968
Site Location: East of East Dereham, on the east side of the A1075 and south of the A47.
Track Status: Dereham Station closed in 1969. Lines lifted.

Although in use for servicing dmus **DEREHAM MPD** still looked very much like a steam shed, with all vents intact, when photographed on March 31st, 1962.

Alec Swain

32A(s) WYMONDHAM

Location: In the fork of the Dereham and Thetford lines, at the west end of Wymondham Station. (OS Map Ref: TG112009)
Directions: Entrance to the shed is effected from the station platform.
Closed: c1958 (Steam), 1974 (Totally)
Description: Consisting of a Turntable, Engine Pit and small Coaling Stage only. There are no shed buildings.
Post Closure History: Lines lifted. Site unused. (1989)

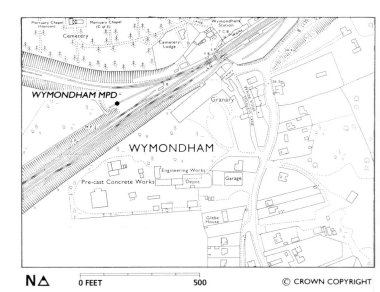

N△   0 FEET   500   © CROWN COPYRIGHT

Map Dated: 1964
Site Location: South of the A47, adjacent to the west side of the B1135.
Track Status: Wymondham Station and Ely to Norwich line are operational.

An 0–6–0 Diesel Shunter is parked over the engine pit at **WYMONDHAM MPD** on May 11th, 1958.

WT Stubbs Collection

32C LOWESTOFT

Location: South of the line, at the junction of the Beccles and Yarmouth lines, west of Lowestoft Central Station. (OS Map Ref: TM536930)

Directions: Turn sharp left outside of the station along Denmark Road. This road follows the line, proceed along it until it begins to bear right. At this point a cinder path, on the left hand side, leads across the lines to the shed.

Closed: July 7th, 1962.

Description: A brick built 4TS dead ended shed.

Post Closure History: Demolished

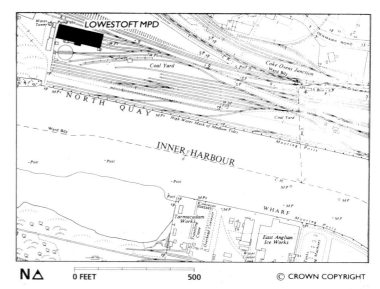

N△   0 FEET   500   © CROWN COPYRIGHT

Map Dated: 1951

Site Location: In the west of the town, on the north bank of Lake Lothing.

Track Status: Lowestoft Station and line are operational.

LOWESTOFT MPD in private use on September 1st, 1968

WT Stubbs Collection

32G MELTON CONSTABLE

Location: On the west side of Melton Constable Station. (OS Map Ref: TG042330)

Directions: Turn left outside the station over the bridge and the shed entrance is on the left hand side.

Closed: February 28th, 1959.

Description: A brick built 3TS dead ended shed.

Post Closure History: Still Standing. In use for industrial purposes (1988)

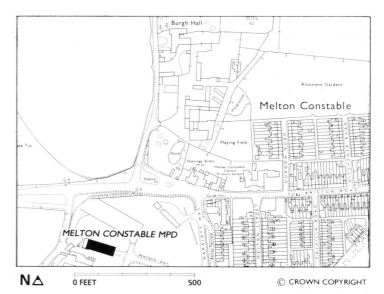

N△   0 FEET   500   © CROWN COPYRIGHT

Map Dated: 1976

Site Location: West of the town centre, south of Briston Road (B1354)

Track Status: Melton Constable Station closed in 1964. Lines lifted.

Ex-LNER Class B17/4 4–6–0 No. 61654 *SUNDERLAND* and ex-LMS Class 4 2–6–0 No. 43159 occupy part of the shed yard at **MELTON CONSTABLE MPD** on February 28th, 1959.   *Sid Nash*

32D YARMOUTH SOUTH TOWN

Location: East of the line, south of Yarmouth South Town Station. (OS Map Ref: TG517068)

Directions: Turn right outside of the station, first right into Station Road and a cinder path leads to the shed from the right hand side of this road.

Closed: November 2nd, 1959

Description: A brick built 2TS through road shed.

Post Closure History: *Demolished. Site redeveloped.*

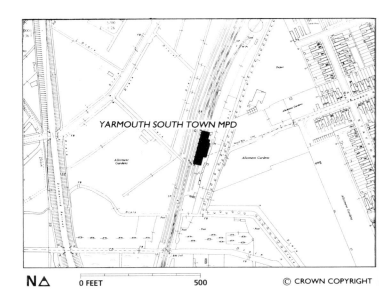

NΔ   0 FEET   500   © CROWN COPYRIGHT

Map Dated: 1964
Site Location: In the south of the town, on the south side of High Mill Road.
Track Status: Yarmouth South Town Station closed in 1970. Lines lifted.

An 0–6–0 diesel locomotive shunts some carriage stock in the shed yard of the closed **YARMOUTH SOUTH TOWN MPD** on August 30th, 1960.
WT Stubbs Collection

32E YARMOUTH VAUXHALL

Location: West of the line, north of Yarmouth Vauxhall Station. (OS Map Ref: TG518082)

Directions: Turn right outside of the station into the Goods Yard and a road runs around the perimeter to the shed.

Closed: January 5th, 1959

Description: A brick built 2TS dead ended shed.

Post Closure History: *Still Standing as recently as 1986. Now demolished and the site is occupied by an Asda Store. (1989)*

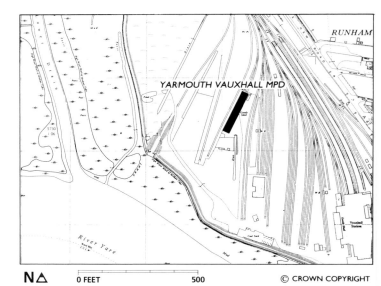

NΔ   0 FEET   500   © CROWN COPYRIGHT

Map Dated: 1964
Site Location: In the east of the town, adjacent to the north side of the River Yare.
Track Status: Yarmouth Vauxhall Station and line are operational.

Ex-LNER Class D16/3 4–4–0 No. 62586 peers out of the shed building at **YARMOUTH VAUXHALL MPD** on September 20th, 1953.   *John Edgington*

32F YARMOUTH BEACH

Location: East of the line, at the north end of Yarmouth Beach Station. (OS Map Ref: TG529082)

Directions: Turn right outside of the station along Nelson Road, first right across the level crossing and the shed entrance is on the right hand side.

Closed: February 28th, 1959.

Description: A brick built 3TS through road shed.

Post Closure History: *Demolished. Now site of Bus Station. (1989)*

A deserted and roofless shed building at **YARMOUTH BEACH MPD**, photographed just after closure in 1959.   *Allan Sommerfield Collection*

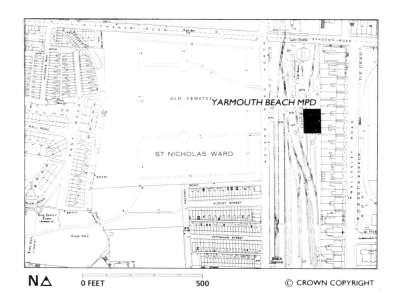

Map Dated: 1951.

Site Location: In the east of the town

Track Status: Yarmouth Beach Station closed in 1959. Lines lifted.

32A(s) SWAFFHAM

Location: South of the line, east of Swaffham Station. (OS Map Ref: TF821095)

Directions: Turn left out of the station along the Station Approach Road. At the end turn left and almost immediately turn right through a gateway. This roadway leads to the shed.

Out of Use: 1960

Description: Latterly consisting of a turntable, engine pit and water tower and column only.

Post Closure History: *Demolished. Site Unused (1972)*

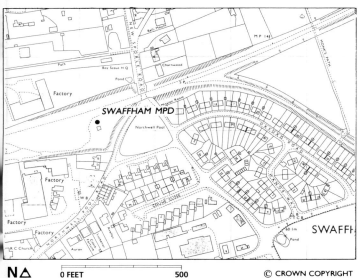

Map Dated: 1970

Site Location: North east of the town centre, east of the A1065.

Track Status: Swaffham Station closed in 1968. Lines lifted.

32A(s) WELLS ON SEA

Location: On the east side of Wells next the Sea Station. (OS Map Ref;TF920433)

Directions: Entrance to the shed is effected from the station platform.

Closed: September 1955.

Description: A brick built 2TS dead ended shed.

Post Closure History: *Demolished. Site of Industrial Development. (1989)*

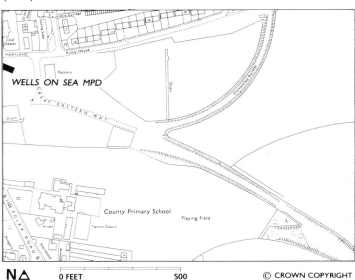

Map Dated: 1973 (Shed Superimposed)

Site Location: South of the town centre, on the east side of Polka Road (B1105) and north of Stiffkey Road (A149)

Track Status: Wells next the Sea Station closed in 1963. Lines lifted.

SUFFOLK

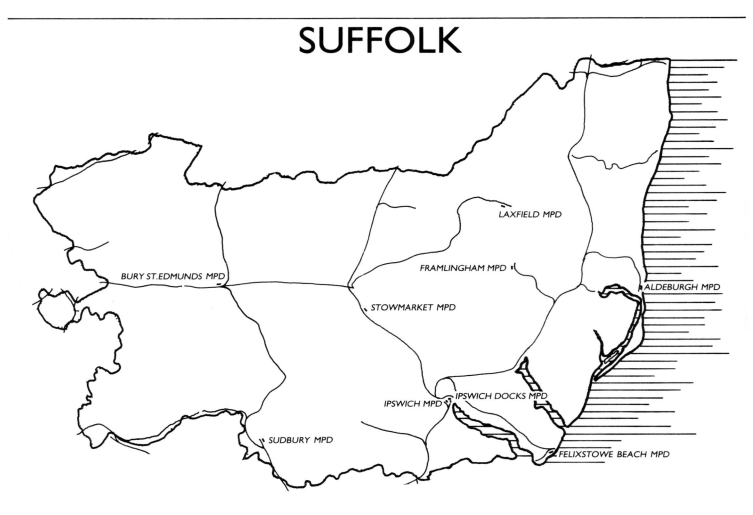

31E(s) SUDBURY

Location: At the end of a short spur in the Goods Yard, on the north side of Sudbury Station.(OS Map Ref: TL876412)

Directions: Turn left outside the station along the Station Drive and right at the end along Great Eastern Road. Cross the small ungated level crossing and turn right through a gate. This leads to the shed in the Goods Yard.

Out of Use: 1959

Description: A brick built ITS dead ended shed.

Post Closure History: Demolished. Floor traceable (1972)

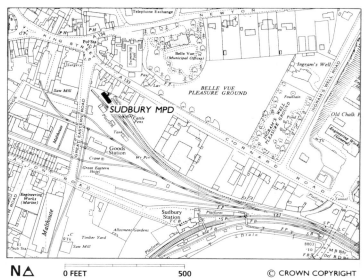

Map Dated: 1956

Site Location: South east of the town centre, on the south side of Cornard Road (A133)

Track Status: Sudbury Station and line east of the station operational.

The shed office was still standing alongside the engine pit at **SUDBURY MPD** on August 31st, 1960. The drums of fuel and small pump alongside the track would indicate that the site was still in use for servicing diesel engines.

WT Stubbs Collection

32B IPSWICH

Location: On the east side of the line, south of Ipswich Station. (OS Map Ref: TM162431)

Directions: Turn right outside the station into Burrell Street, fork right into Willoughby Road and turn left at the top of the hill into Belstead Road. Turn right into Rectory Road, left into Croft Street, right at the end into Wherstead Road, and the shed entrance is on the right hand side.

Closed: November 2nd, 1959 (Steam), 1968 (Totally)

Description: Completely rebuilt in 1954 into a concrete 6TS through road shed.

Post Closure History: Still Standing. Upon closure converted for use as a diesel depot and subsequently closed. (1988)

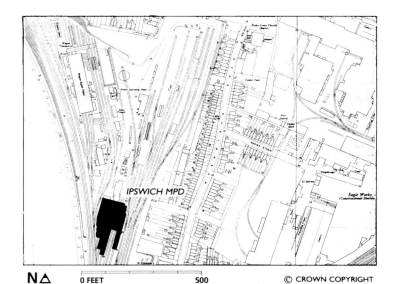

N△ 0 FEET   500   © CROWN COPYRIGHT

Map Dated: 1952 (Showing shed prior to rebuilding)
Site Location: In the south of the town, on the west side of the A137.
Track Status: Ipswich Station and line are operational.

IPSWICH MPD, as rebuilt in 1954 and complete with coaling stage, photographed on September 2nd, 1960, just after total dieselisation.   *WT Stubbs Collection*

32B(s) IPSWICH DOCKS

Location: On a spur in Ipswich Docks. (OS Map Ref: TM162440)

Directions: Go straight ahead outside Ipswich Station, into Princes Street, turn right into Commercial Road and right again into the Goods Yard, by the junction with St.Peter's Street. The shed is inside this yard on the right hand side just past the Goods Station.

Out of Use: 1955

Description: A corrugated iron 1TS dead ended shed.

Post Closure History: Demolished. Now site of sidings. (1989)

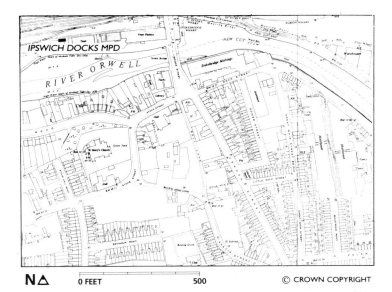

N△ 0 FEET   500   © CROWN COPYRIGHT

Map Dated: 1952
Site Location: In the south of the town, on the north bank of the River Orwell.
Track Status: Docks Branch operational.

The diminutive and life-expired **IPSWICH DOCKS MPD**, known as the 'Tram Shed' it housed one of the famous ex-LNER Class J70 0–6–0 Tram Locos, complete with protective 'skirt' for working through the streets.
Allan Sommerfield Collection

32B(s) ALDEBURGH

Location: East of the line, at the north end of Aldeburgh Station. (OS Map Ref: TM459572)

Directions: Entrance to the shed is effected from the station platform.

Out of Use: April 1955.

Description: A brick built 2TS through road shed.

Post Closure History: *Demolished. The shed site and a large part of the station area is occupied by a housing estate.*

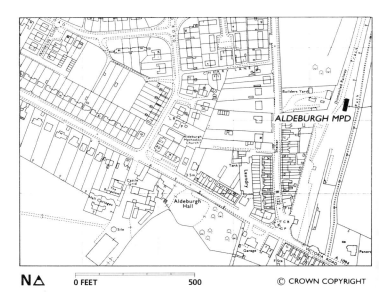

NA △   0 FEET   500   © CROWN COPYRIGHT

Map Dated: 1971 (Shed Superimposed)

Site Location: On the north side of Victoria Road (A1094) in the north of the town.

Track Status: Aldeburgh Station closed in 1966. Lines lifted.

A vintage shot of **ALDEBURGH MPD** with LNER Class F3 2–4–2T No. 8073 parked in the entrance on May 17th, 1937.   *Allan Sommerfield Collection*

32B(s) LAXFIELD

Location: South of the line, west of Laxfield Station. (OS Map Ref: TM287723)

Directions: Entrance to the shed is effected from the station platform.

Closed: July 28th, 1952 (Line Closure Date)

Description: A wooden built 1TS dead ended shed.

Post Closure History: *Demolished. Site now in agricultural use. (1989)*

A classic pre-war view of the wooden shed at **LAXFIELD MPD** with LNER Class J65 0–6–0T No. 7253 *(Later BR No. 68215)* parked on the shed road on July 5th, 1936.   *Allan Sommerfield Collection*

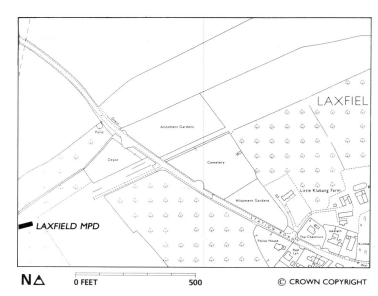

NA △   0 FEET   500   © CROWN COPYRIGHT

Map Dated: 1981 (Shed Superimposed)

Site Location: North west of the town centre, on the west side of Station Road (B1117)

Track Status: Laxfield Station closed in 1952. Lines lifted.

32B(s) FELIXSTOWE

Location: On the west side of the line, at the north end of Felixstowe Beach Station. (OS Map Ref: TM294341)
Directions: Entrance to the shed is effected from the station platform.
Closed: January 5th, 1959. *(Considered as a Signing-on Point only from c1950)*
Description: Originally a 2TS shed, by BR days the depot consisted of two tracks with engine pits and watering facility.
Post Closure History: Lines lifted

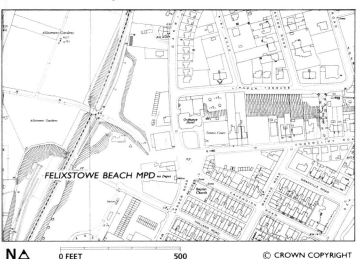

N△ 0 FEET 500 © CROWN COPYRIGHT

Map Dated: 1953
Site Location: South west of the town centre, west of the A45
Track Status: Felixstowe Beach Station closed in 1967.

A turntable and watering facility also existed at Felixstowe Town Station and was used by visiting steam locomotives during the 1950s.

32B(s) FRAMLINGHAM

Location: West of the line, south of Framlingham Station. (OS Map Ref: TM284627)
Directions: Entrance to the shed is effected from the station platform.
Closed: November 3rd, 1952
Description: A brick built 1TS dead ended shed.
Post Closure History: Demolished. Now site of Industrial Development. (1978)

Ex-LNER Class J15 0–6–0 No. 65467 sits alongside the water tower at **FRAMLINGHAM MPD**   *Allan Sommerfield Collection*

32B(s) STOWMARKET

Location: East of the line, at the south end of the Goods Yard, south of Stowmarket Station. (OS Map Ref;TM054585)
Directions: Entrance to the shed is effected from the station platform
Closed: 1960 (Steam), 1975 (Totally)
Description: Consisting solely of an engine pit and offices.
Post Closure History: Lines lifted.

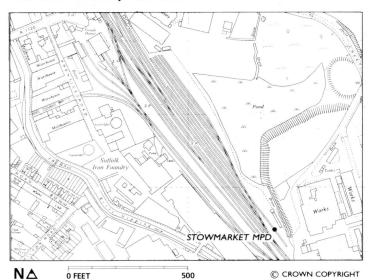

N△ 0 FEET 500 © CROWN COPYRIGHT

Map Dated: 1968
Site Location: East of the River Gipping, south of Stowupland Road (A1120).
Track Status: Stowmarket Station and line are operational.

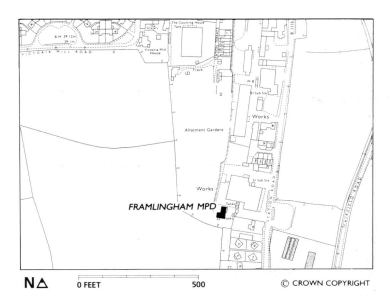

N△ 0 FEET 500 © CROWN COPYRIGHT

Map Dated: 1978 (Shed Superimposed)
Site Location: In the south of the town, adjacent to the west side of Station Road (B1116)
Track Status: Framlingham Station closed in 1952. Lines lifted

31E BURY ST.EDMUNDS

Location: North of the line, west of Bury St.Edmunds Station. (OS Map Ref: TL849652)

Directions: Turn left outside of the station, left under the bridge and left again into the Goods Yard. A path leads to the shed through this yard.

Closed: January 5th, 1959 (Steam)

Description: A brick built 3TS through road shed.

Post Closure History: Demolished. Floors traceable. Site unused. (1989)

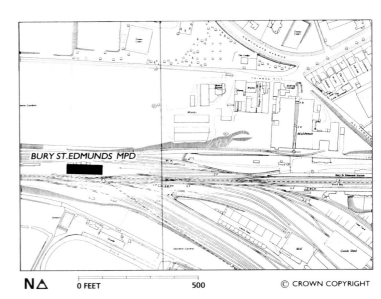

N△   0 FEET   500   © CROWN COPYRIGHT

Map Dated: 1966

Site Location: In the north of the town, west of the A134.

Track Status: Bury St.Edmunds Station and line are operational.

Ex-LNER Class B12 4–6–0 No. 61555 heads a line of locomotives in **BURY ST.ED-MUNDS MPD** on May 26th, 1957.
Ken Fairey

The debate as to when is a shed a shed, or a stabling point a stabling point *(See Volume 1, Page 6)* is epitomised in this photograph of the locomotive sidings at CHINGFORD. With Stabling Roads, Engine Pit, Coaling and Watering Facilities it would appear to have every credential to qualify, at the very least, as a Stabling Point. However it was never "listed" and, like many other similar sites, retained "official" anonymity throughout its existence.
Alec Swain

CAMBRIDGESHIRE

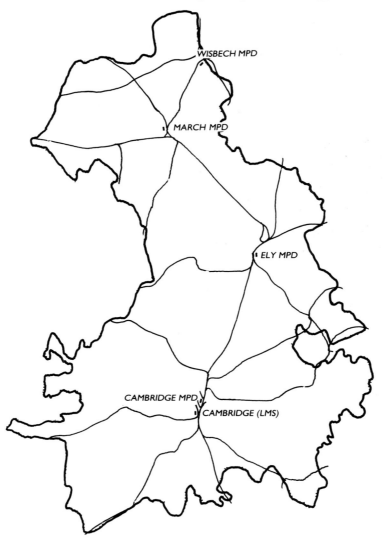

31A(s) ELY

Location: East of the line, south of Ely Station. (OS Map Ref: TL542791)
Directions: Entrance to the shed is effected from the station platform.
Out of Use: 1962
Description: Originally a corrugated iron ITS shed, but latterly, following demolition, locomotives stabled alongside the water tower.
Post Closure History: *Lines lifted*

Ex-LNER Class J17 0–6–0 No. 65582 stands over the engine pit that constituted **ELY MPD** on February 19th, 1961. *Ken Fairey*

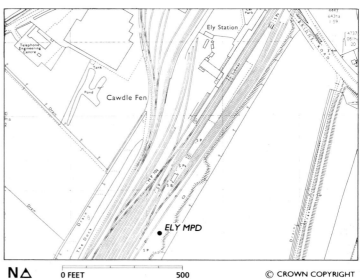

Map Dated: 1971
Site Location: South east of the town centre, on the south side of Bridge Road (A142)
Track Status: Ely Station and lines are operational.

31A CAMBRIDGE

Location: On the west side of the line at the north end of Cambridge Station. (OS Map Ref: TL462574)
Directions: The shed entrance is in the station yard.
Closed: June 18th, 1962.
Description: A brick built 7TS dead ended shed.
Post Closure History: *Demolished, the whole site is now the station car park. (1989)*

A general view of **CAMBRIDGE MPD** on September 4th, 1960.
WT Stubbs Collection

4A(s) CAMBRIDGE (LMS)

Location: West of the line, south of Cambridge Station. (OS Map Ref: TL460568)
Directions: Leave the station by the approach road and turn left along Hills Road. The entrance to the Goods Yard is on the right hand side, just before the railway bridge, and a pathway leads to the shed through this yard.
Closed: December 2nd, 1935, and subsequently used as a stabling point until about 1951.
Description: A brick built 2TS dead ended shed. By BR days locomotives were turned and stabled in the yard only.
Post Closure History: *Demolished 1964. Site Unused. (1989)*

A rare view of **CAMBRIDGE (LMS) MPD** taken in November, 1938. It was already closed by this date and by BR days locomotives were turned on the shed turntable and serviced on adjacent tracks. *Bernard Matthews Collection*

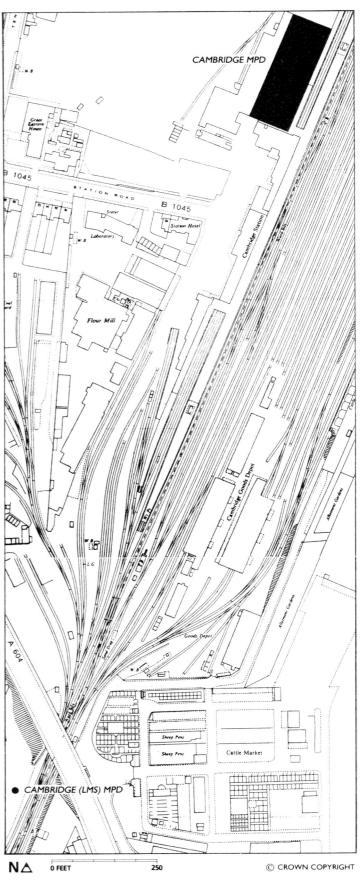

N△ 0 FEET 250 © CROWN COPYRIGHT

Map Dated: 1969
Site Location: Cambridge Station is south east of the town centre, east of Hills Road (A604)
Track Status: Cambridge Station and line are operational

31B MARCH

Location: On the west side of the March to Spalding line, north of March Station. (OS Map Ref: TL412985)

Directions: Turn left outside of the station, left over the level crossing and first left into Norwood Road. A broad cinder path leads to the shed from the right hand side of this road, just past the railway bridge.

Closed: December 1963 (Steam)

Description: Composed of brick built 10TS and 5TS through road sheds.

Post Closure History: Partially demolished and replaced by a purpose built diesel depot. (Code MR)

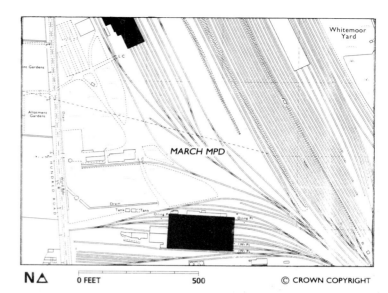

Map Dated: 1970
Site Location: North west of the town centre, west of the B1101.
Track Status: Lines operational

The transition from steam to diesel was well under way at **MARCH MPD** when photographed on August 29th, 1960.   *WT Stubbs Collection*

31C(s) WISBECH

Location: On the south side of Wisbech East Station. (OS Map Ref: TF461089)

Directions: Entrance to the shed is effected from the level crossing at the west end of the station.

Closed: March 1953 (Steam): May 23rd, 1966 (Totally)

Description: A brick built 2TS dead ended shed.

Post Closure History: Rebuilt as a 1TS shed to accomodate the diesel shunters. Demolished after total closure and is now the site of private dwellings. (1989)

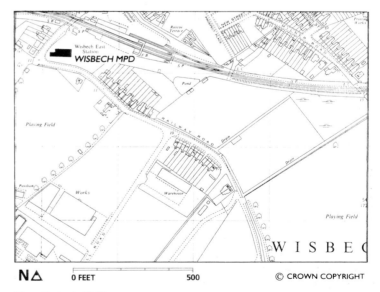

Map Dated: 1969
Site Location: In the south of the town, east of the A1101.
Track Status: Wisbech East Station closed in 1968. Lines lifted.

0–6–0 Diesel Shunter No. 11101 nestles inside the shed building at **WISBECH MPD** on March 16th, 1958.   *Allan Sommerfield Collection*

PART SIX
CENTRAL ENGLAND

**WORCESTERSHIRE HUNTINGDON SHROPSHIRE   WARWICKSHIRE
HEREFORDSHIRE   WEST MIDLANDS   NORTHAMPTONSHIRE**

WORCESTERSHIRE

21B(s) REDDITCH

Location: West of the line, north of Redditch Station.(OS Map Ref: SP039681)

Directions: Bear left outside of the station across Unicorn Hill and proceed along Windsor Street. Continue along Hewell Road and turn right into Clive Road. A gate on the left hand side leads into a small Goods Yard and the shed is on the opposite side of the line.

Closed: June 1st 1964.

Description: A brick built 1TS dead ended shed.

Post Closure History: Demolished. Site Unused. (1989)

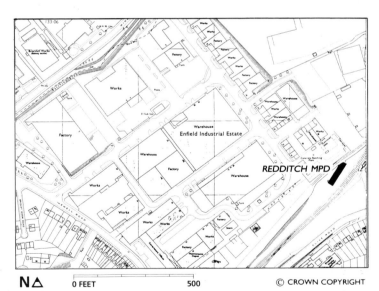

Map Dated: 1978 (Shed Superimposed)

Site Location: In the north of the town, west of the A441.

Track Status: Redditch Station and line are operational.

Ex-LMS Class 4 2-6-0 No. 43010 stands in the tiny shed yard at **REDDITCH MPD** on July 5th, 1959.
WT Stubbs

21C BROMSGROVE

Location: On the east side of the line at the south end of Bromsgrove Station. (OS Map Ref: SO968697)
Directions: A path runs from the southbound platform to the shed.
Closed: September 27th, 1964.
Description: A brick built 3TS shed with 1 through road.
Post Closure History: The locoshed and adjacent Wagon Works were demolished and the whole site is now a housing estate.(1989)

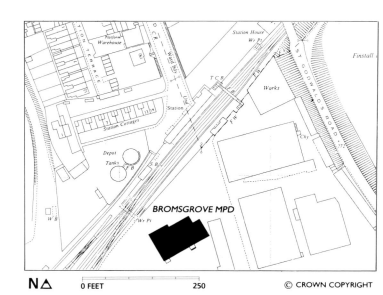

Ex-GWR 0–6–0PT and Ex-LMS Jinty 0–6–0T locomotives take a breather from their banking duties on the Lickey Incline. **BROMSGROVE MPD** on July 5th, 1959.
WT Stubbs Collection

Map Dated: 1967
Site Location: About 1 mile east of Bromsgrove, on the south side of Finstall Road.
Track Status: Bromsgrove Station and line are operational.

85A WORCESTER

Location: In the triangle of lines from Foregate Street to Droitwich to Shrub Hill, north of Worcester Shrub Hill Station. (OS Map Ref: SO857556)
Directions: Turn right outside of the station along a footpath running parallel to the line, descend the flight of steps and turn left into Tolladine Road. A footpath leads to the shed from the right hand side, about 50 yards further on.
Closed: December 1965.
Description: A complex consisting of a brick built through road 4TS and 3TS sheds.
Post Closure History: Used as a diesel depot (Code WS) for some time. The freight engine shed remains intact, but roofless. The passenger engine shed which had been roofless for years is now demolished. (1987)

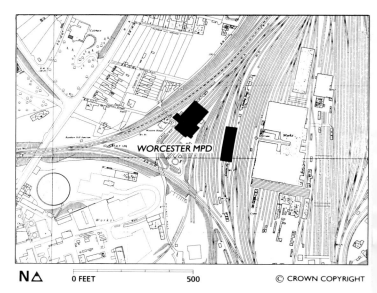

Ex-GWR Castle Class 4–6–0 No. 7013 *BRISTOL CASTLE* stands in the entrance to the three track straighthouse at **WORCESTER MPD** on September 9th, 1962.
WT Stubbs Collection

Map Dated: 1965
Site Location: East of the town centre, on the north side of Tolladine Road.
Track Status: Worcester Shrub Hill Station and lines are operational.

85A(s) EVESHAM

Location: In the fork of the Oxford and Stratford upon Avon lines, west of Evesham Station. (OS Map Ref: SP033447)
Directions: There is no definite pathway. Entrance to the shed is effected from the station platform.
Closed: June 1961
Description: A brick built 1TS through road shed.
Post Closure History: Demolished. Site Unused. (1989)

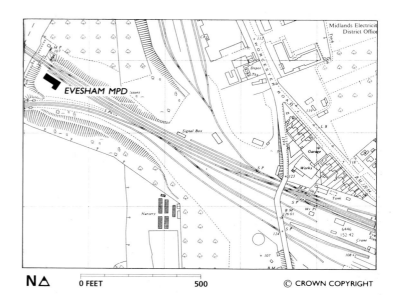

Map Dated: 1968
Site Location: North of the town centre, west of the A435.
Track Status: Evesham Station and Worcester to Oxford line are operational.

Ex-GWR 4300 Class 2–6–0 No. 6388 sits in the entrance to **EVESHAM MPD** in a view taken in the late 1950s.
Bill Potter

85A(s) HONEYBOURNE

Location: North of the line, at the west end of Honeybourne Station. (OS Map Ref: SP113449)
Directions: Entrance to the shed is effected from the station platform.
Closed: December 1965.
Description: Consisting of a single track and engine pit. There are no Shed Buildings.
Post Closure History: Lines lifted and pit filled in. Site Unused (1972)

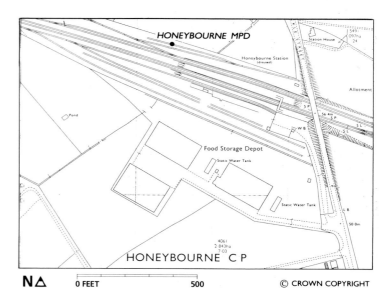

Map Dated: 1971
Site Location: North of Church Honeybourne, on the west side of Buckle Street *(part of Ryknild Street, a Roman road)*
Track Status: Honeybourne Station and line are operational.

Ex-GWR 2251 Class 0–6–0 No. 2289 stands at the coaling stage and engine pit that constituted **HONEYBOURNE MPD** on June 26th, 1960
Ken Fairey

85D KIDDERMINSTER

Location: On the south side of the Bewdley line, south of Kidderminster Station. (OS Map Ref: SO832751)

Directions: Turn sharp right out of the station yard into Comberton Road, turn first right into Farfield, right at the end into the main road and right into a cinder path. Proceed over the footbridge and turn left into Hoo Road. A cinder path leads to the shed from the right hand side of this pathway.

Closed: August 10th, 1964.

Description: A corrugated iron 2TS dead ended shed.

Post Closure History: Demolished, the site is now a housing estate.(1989)

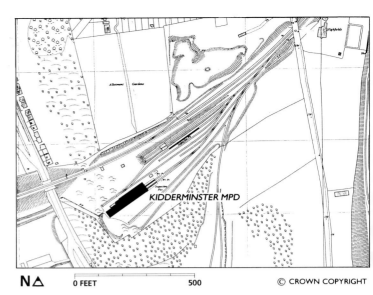

The sun beams through the roof on a hazy April day in 1962 at **KIDDERMINSTER MPD**   *WT Stubbs*

N△   0 FEET   500   © CROWN COPYRIGHT

Map Dated: 1954

Site Location: South east of the town centre, adjacent to the east side of Worcester Road (A442)

Track Status: Kidderminster Station and lines are operational.

The Kidderminster to Bewdley line is preserved as part of the Severn Valley Railway

As mentioned on Page 18, the shed buildings at **NORWICH CITY MPD** were dismantled and removed by the North Norfolk Railway for their own use and this view, taken on September 6th, 1989, shows ex-GER Class J15 0–6–0 No. 564 *(BR No.65462)* at the newly re-erected depot at **WEYBOURNE**.   *Ken Fairey*

HUNTINGDON

31A(s) HUNTINGDON EAST

Location: North of the line, at the east end of Huntingdon East Station. (OS Map Ref: TL234715)
Directions: Entrance to the shed is effected from the station platform.
Out of Use: 1959
Description: A brick built 1TS dead ended shed.
Post Closure History: *Demolished. Part of the station site is now a car park, the remainder, including the shed and turntable pit, is a horses paddock. (1989)*

The compact layout at **HUNTINGDON EAST MPD**
Allan Sommerfield Collection

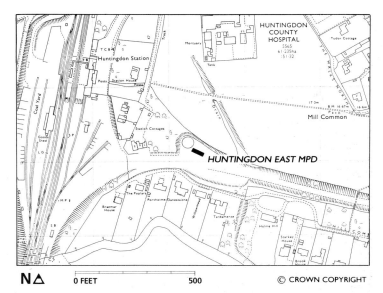

Map Dated: 1971 (Shed Superimposed)
Site Location: On the west side of the town, adjacent to the south side of the A604. The A14 bypass follows part of the old trackbed and is immediately north of the shed site.
Track Status: Huntingdon East Station closed in 1959. Lines lifted. Huntingdon Station and line are operational.

SHROPSHIRE

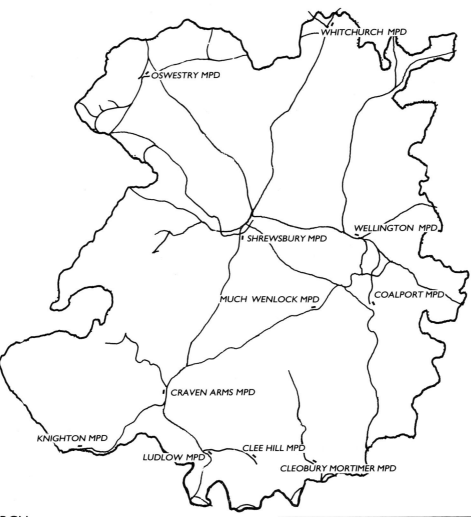

5A(s) WHITCHURCH

Location: East of the line, at the north end of Whitchurch Station. (OS Map Ref: SJ551415)

Directions: Turn left outside of the station along the approach road, left again under the bridge and left again along a cinder path running parallel to the line. A path on the left hand side leads to the shed.

Closed: September 1957.

Description: A brick built 4TS dead ended shed.

Post Closure History: Demolished.

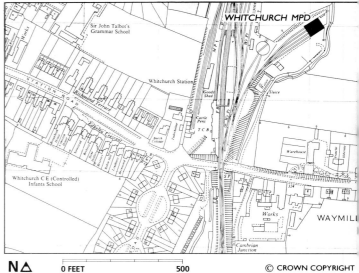

Map Dated: 1964

Site Location: North east of the town centre, north of Station Road (A525)

Track Status: Whitchurch Station and line are operational.

A distant view of **WHITCHURCH MPD** on April 6th, 1955.   *John Edgington*

84G SHREWSBURY

Location: On the east side of the Hereford line, south of Shrewsbury Station. (OS Map Ref: SJ500119)

Directions: Turn left outside of the station along Castle Gates, proceed along Castle Street, turn left into St.Marys Street, continue along Dogpole, turn left into Wyle Cop, cross the English Bridge and turn right along Coleham Head. Fork left into Betton Street, turn left into Scott Street and the shed entrance is a door on the left hand side.

Closed: March 6th, 1967.

Description: A large shed area consisting of a brick built roundhouse and brick built 8TS and 9TS dead ended straighthouses.

Post Closure History: *Demolished. Site Unused. (1989)*

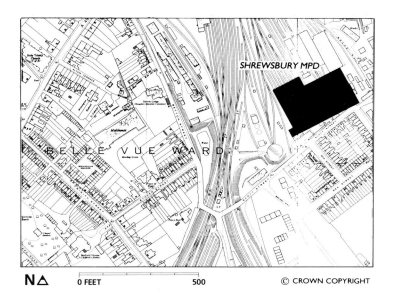

N△   0 FEET   500   © CROWN COPYRIGHT

Map Dated: 1964

Site Location: In the south of the town, on the east side of Belle Vue Road (A49)

Track Status: Shrewsbury Station and line are operational.

The ex-LMS portion of **SHREWSBURY MPD** photographed on July 5th, 1959.
WT Stubbs

84G(s) CLEE HILL

Location: On the south side of the Clee Hill branch, a short distance east of the top of the incline. (OS Map Ref:SO589760)

Directions: From the junction of Dhustone Lane and the A4117, about one mile west of Clee Hill: Proceed northwards along Dhustone Lane and turn right along a pathway, just before the railway bridge. This pathway runs parallel to the line and the shed is on the left hand side about 300 yards along.

Closed: November 14th, 1960

Description: A wooden built 1TS dead ended shed.

Post Closure History: *Demolished. Site is now used for grazing cattle. (1989)*

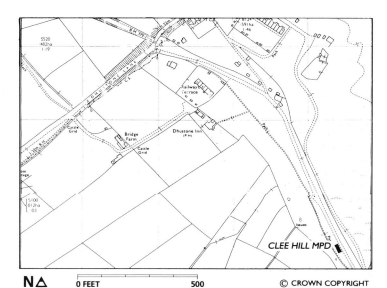

N△   0 FEET   500   © CROWN COPYRIGHT

Map Dated: 1970

Track Status: All lines lifted

The heavily-buttressed wooden built **CLEE HILL MPD** on April 3rd, 1955.
John Edgington

85D(s) CLEOBURY MORTIMER

Location: East of the line, north of Cleobury Town Station. (OS Map Ref: SO680772)
Directions: Entrance to the shed is effected from the station platform.
Closed: July 1938. Used as a Stabling Point until 1965
Description: A concrete built 1TS dead ended shed.
Post Closure History: Still standing, in a totally derelict condition. (1989)

A pre-war view of **CLEOBURY MORTIMER MPD** taken on September 24th, 1938.   *Allan Sommerfield Collection*

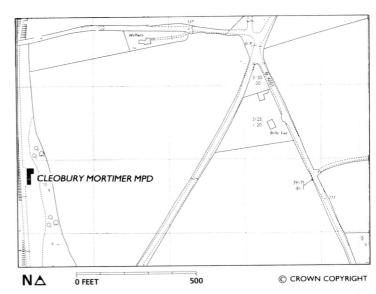

Map Dated: 1969
Site Location: About 1 mile north east of Cleobury Mortimer on the north side of the B4363.
Track Status: Cleobury Town Station closed in 1938. Lines lifted.
The shed building was reported as having been struck by lightning after abandonment.

84G(s) COALPORT

Location: North of the line, at the east end of Coalport (LNWR) Station.(OS Map Ref: SJ702021)
Directions: Entrance to the shed is effected from the station platform.
Closed: May 31st, 1952.
Description: A brick built 1TS dead ended shed.
Post Closure History: Demolished. Site Unused (1974)

COALPORT MPD appeared to be remarkably intact despite nine years of closure when photographed on May 22nd, 1961.   *WT Stubbs Collection*

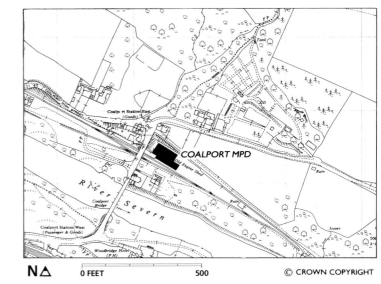

Map Dated: 1957
Site Location: In the centre of the town, on the north bank of the River Severn.
Track Status: Coalport (LNWR) Station closed in 1952. Lines lifted.

84G(s) CRAVEN ARMS

Location: On the west side of the line at the north end of Craven Arms & Stokesay Station. (OS Map Ref: SO431833)
Directions: Entrance to the shed is effected from the station platform.
Closed: c1965.
Description: A brick built 4TS dead ended shed.
Post Closure History: Demolished. Site Unused.

A quiet moment at **CRAVEN ARMS MPD** on July 5th, 1959.

WT Stubbs Collection

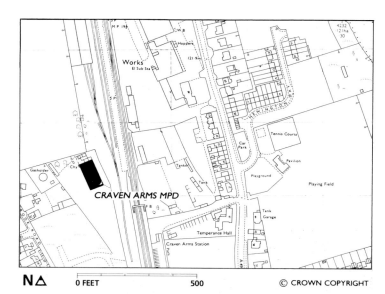

Map Dated: 1975
Site Location: North of the town, west of the A49
Track Status: Craven Arms Station and line are operational.

84G(s) KNIGHTON

Location: North of the line, east of Knighton Station. (OS Map Ref: SO295724)
Directions: Turn right outside of the station, cross the railway bridge and turn right along the roadway. The shed entrance is a gate on the right hand side a short distance along.
Closed: January 1st, 1962.
Description: A stone built 1TS through road shed.
Post Closure History: Demolished. Site Unused. (1989)

An ex-LMS Class 8F 2–8–0 stands in the shed yard at **KNIGHTON MPD** on May 21st, 1961.

WT Stubbs Collection

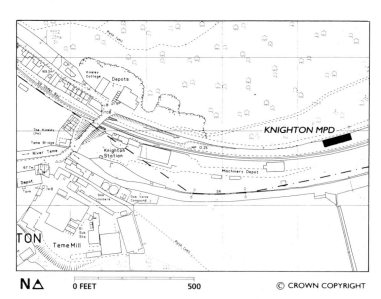

Map Dated: 1977 (Shed Superimposed)
Site Location: In the east of the town, on the north bank of the River Teme.
Track Status: Knighton Station and line are operational.

84G(s) LUDLOW

Location: In a small goods yard, east of the line, north of Ludlow Station. (OS Map Ref: SO513752)

Directions: Entrance to the shed is effected from the station platform.

Closed: December 29th 1951.

Description: A brick built 1TS through road shed

Post Closure History: Still Standing. In use as part of a motor vehicle garage premises. (1989)

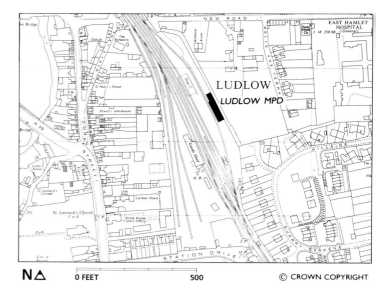

Map Dated: 1968

Site Location: North east of the town centre, on the south side of New Road (A4117)

Track Status: Ludlow Station and line are operational.

Although the line into the shed had been lifted, **LUDLOW MPD** still looked in pretty good shape when photographed on July 5th, 1959.   *WT Stubbs*

84H WELLINGTON

Location: North of the line, at the east end of Wellington Station. (OS Map Ref:SJ652117)

Directions: Leave the station, ascend the steps and turn left along a road running parallel to the line. Turn left at the end into Victoria Street, cross the bridge and the shed entrance is on the left hand side.

Closed: August 10th, 1964.

Description: A brick built 3TS shed with one through road.

Post Closure History: Demolished. Site Unused. (1989)

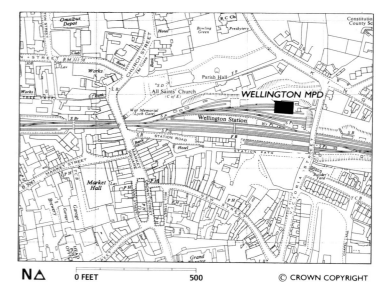

Map Dated: 1959

Site Location: In the centre of Telford New Town, on the west side of King Street.

Track Status: Wellington Station and line are operational.

WELLINGTON MPD plays host to a trio of pannier tanks on May 1st, 1957.   *John Edgington*

84H(s) MUCH WENLOCK

Location: East of the line, south of Much Wenlock Station. (OS Map Ref: SJ621008)

Directions: Turn left outside of the station along Station Road, turn left into Sheinton Street and almost immediately right along New Road. The entrance to the small Goods Yard is on the right hand side, and the shed is within this yard.

Closed: December 31st, 1951.

Description: A brick built 1TS dead ended shed.

Post Closure History: *Demolished. The whole site is now a Housing Estate. (1989)*

MUCH WENLOCK MPD on May 22nd, 1961.   *WT Stubbs Collection*

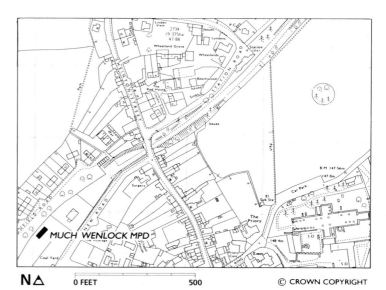

Map Dated: 1972 (Shed Superimposed)
Site Location: In the north west of the town.
Track Status: Much Wenlock Station closed in 1962. Lines lifted.

89A OSWESTRY

Location: In the fork of the Whitchurch and Gobowen lines, east of Oswestry Station. (OS Map Ref: SJ298302)

Directions: Turn right outside of the station and left along the side of the Goods Yard. Turn right into Beatrice Street, proceed along Gobowen Road, fork right into Whittington Road, pass under the bridge and the shed entrance is on the right hand side.

Closed: January 18th, 1965.

Description: A brick built 6TS shed with one through road.

Post Closure History: *Still Standing (1987)*

Ex-GWR Manor Class 4-6-0 No. 7819 *HINTON MANOR* standing in the shed yard at **OSWESTRY MPD** on July 19th, 1953.   *Bill Potter*

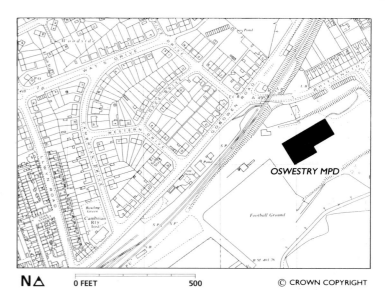

Map Dated: 1970
Site Location: North east of town centre, immediately east of Whittington Road (A495)
Track Status: Oswestry Station closed in 1966. Some lines lifted.

WARWICKSHIRE

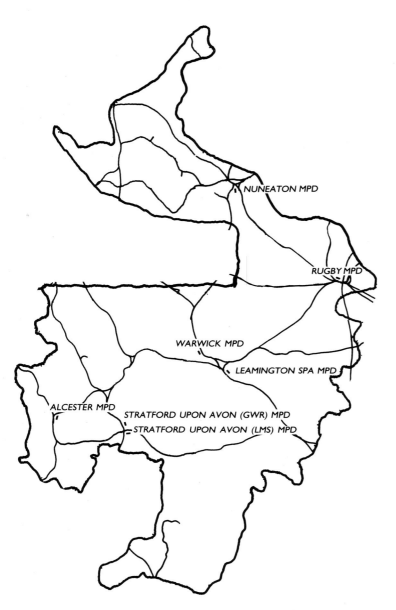

2A RUGBY

Location: On the east side of Rugby Midland Station. (OS Map Ref: SP512760)

Directions: Turn left outside of the station, left under the bridge and a gate on the right hand side leads to the shed via a wooden ramp.

Closed: May 25th, 1965.

Description: A brick built 22TS dead ended shed.

Post Closure History: *No.2 Shed (12TS) was demolished in 1960 for use as a Car Park. The entire site is now in use as an Industrial Development, with a 'Grundig' depot occupying most of the original shed area. (1988)*

A smattering of diesel locomotives and dmus occupy the large shed at **RUGBY MPD** on July 18th, 1965. *WT Stubbs Collection*

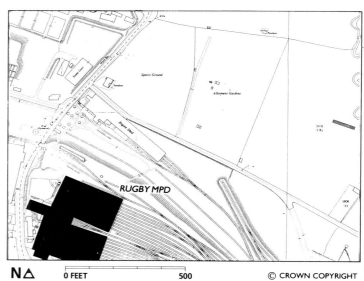

RUGBY MPD

N△ 0 FEET   500   © CROWN COPYRIGHT

Map Dated: 1959

Site Location: In the north of the town.

Track Status: Rugby Midland Station and line are operational.

The purpose-built Diesel and Electric Depot, sited north of the steam shed buildings, is still standing, in use for permanent way engineering.

2B NUNEATON

Location: In the fork of the main and Coventry lines, south of Nuneaton Trent Valley Station. (OS Map Ref: SP369917)

Directions: Leave the station by means of the west exit into Broad Street, turn left into Regent Street, left at the end into Wheat Street and right into Glebe Road. Turn left at the end into a broad drive and a boarded crossing leads over the lines to the shed.

Closed: June 6th, 1966.

Description: A brick built 8TS dead ended shed.

Post Closure History: Demolished

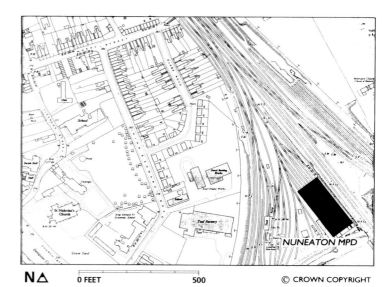

Map Dated: 1954

Site Location: East of the town centre, east of Church Street (B4114)

Track Status: Nuneaton Station and main line are operational.

NUNEATON MPD under the shadow of total electrification of the WCML alongside on October 7th, 1962.
WT Stubbs Collection

2C WARWICK

Location: West of the line, north of Warwick (Milverton) Station. (OS Map Ref: SP304661)

Directions: Leave the station by means of the New Road exit, turn left almost immediately into a footpath and left again into Rugby Road. Pass under the bridge, turn right into Old Milverton Road and the shed entrance is on the right hand side.

Closed: November 17th, 1958.

Description: A brick built 6TS dead ended shed.

Post Closure History: Used as a water garden centre after closure, although the walls had been demolished and the pits were in use as fish tanks! Now totally demolished and the site is occupied by a housing estate. (1989)

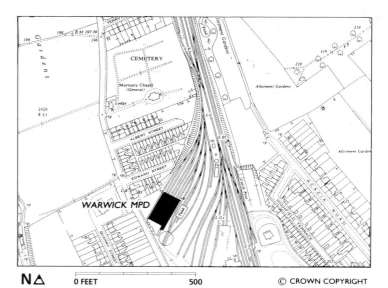

Map Dated: 1953

Site Location: North east of Warwick town centre, on the north side of the A445

Track Status: Warwick (Milverton) Station closed in 1965. Line operational

WARWICK MILVERTON MPD on April 25th, 1954.
Allan Sommerfield Collection

84D LEAMINGTON SPA

Location: East of the line, south of Leamington Spa Station. (OS Map Ref: SP326648)

Directions: Turn left outside of the station into Old Warwick Road, proceed along High Street and Radford Road and then turn right into Camberwell Terrace. Pass under the two railway bridges, enter Warneford Place and a cinder path, running from a gate on the left hand side, leads to the shed.

Closed: June 14th, 1965.

Description: A brick built 4TS dead ended shed.

Post Closure History: *Demolished The site is now part of an Industrial Estate. (1989)*

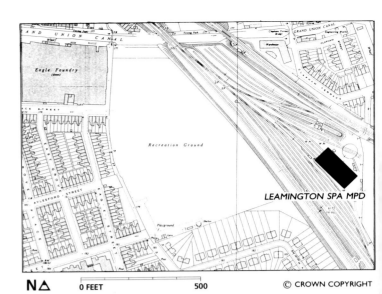

Map Dated: 1952

Site Location: East of the town centre, on the south side of the Grand Union Canal.

Track Status: Leamington Station and ex-GWR line operational. Ex-LMS lines lifted.

LEAMINGTON SPA MPD on September 18th, 1963.   *WT Stubbs Collection*

84D(s) ALCESTER

Location: On the east side of the junction of the Redditch and Bearley lines, north of Alcester Station. (OS Map Ref: SP083581)

Directions: Entrance to the shed is effected from the station platform.

Closed: October 27th, 1939 and subsequently used as a Stabling Point until March 1st, 1951.

Description: A brick built 1TS dead ended shed.

Post Closure History: *Demolished. The shed site and most of the line in the area of the station is occupied by a housing estate. (1989)*

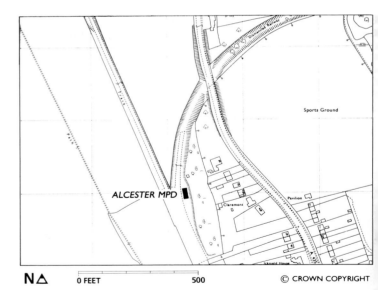

Map Dated: 1971 (Shed Superimposed)

Site Location: In the north of the town, on the west side of the A435.

Track Status: Alcester Station closed in 1962. Lines lifted.

ALCESTER MPD in 1953. Although closed in 1939 the facilities at the derelict shed had been used for servicing locomotives until closure of the Bearley branch in 1951.   *Allan Sommerfield Collection*

21D STRATFORD UPON AVON (LMS)

Location: On the south side of Stratford upon Avon (LMS) Station. (OS Map Ref: SP199540)
Directions: Entrance to the shed is effected from the station platform.
Closed: July 22nd, 1957.
Description: A brick built 4TS dead ended shed.
Post Closure History: *Demolished. Site Unused (1975)*

Ex-LMS 0–6–0 No. 44391 occupies the shed yard at **STRATFORD UPON AVON LMS MPD**, just two months before closure in May 1957.
Allan Sommerfield Collection

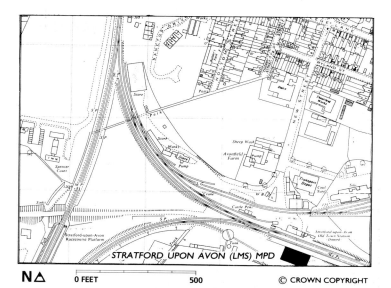

N△   0 FEET   500   © CROWN COPYRIGHT

STRATFORD UPON AVON (LMS) MPD

Map Dated: 1965 (Shed Superimposed)
Site Location: South west of the town centre, on the south side of the A439.
Track Status: Stratford upon Avon (LMS) Station closed in 1952. Lines lifted.

84E(s) STRATFORD UPON AVON (GWR)

Location: East of the line, north of Stratford upon Avon (GWR) Station. (OS Map Ref: SP196554)
Directions: A gate in the station yard leads to the shed.
Closed: September 10th, 1962.
Description: A brick built 2TS dead ended shed.
Post Closure History: *Demolished. Site Unused. (1989)*

Ex-GWR 2200 Class 0–6–0 No. 2211 stands outside the shed at **STRATFORD UPON AVON GWR MPD** on May 15th, 1960.   *Ken Fairey*

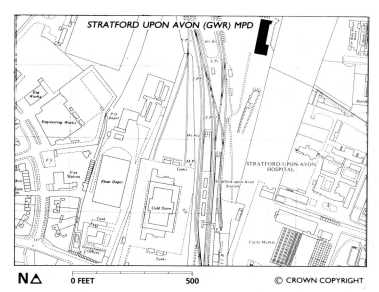

STRATFORD UPON AVON (GWR) MPD

N△   0 FEET   500   © CROWN COPYRIGHT

Map Dated: 1967
Site Location: West of town centre, north of the A422.
Track Status: Stratford upon Avon (GWR) Station and line north of station operational.

HEREFORDSHIRE

85C HEREFORD

Location: On the west side of the Hereford avoiding line (goods) by Barton Goods Yard.(OS Map Ref:SO503398)

Directions: Turn left outside Hereford Station along Station Road, turn right into Commercial Road and continue along High Town, High Street and Eign Street. Turn left into Victoria Road, right into Barton Street and continue into Barton Road. The shed entrance is a gate on the right hand side, just past the bridge.

Closed: November 2nd, 1964.

Description: A stone built 8TS shed with 4 through roads.

Post Closure History: Demolished. Site now occupied by Council Road Transport Depot. (1987)

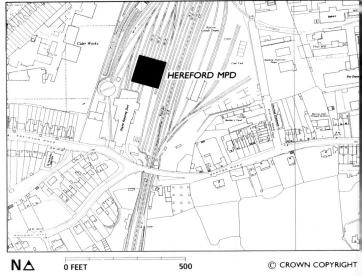

Map Dated: 1967

Site Location: In the west of the town, adjacent to the east side of Bulmers Cider Works.

Track Status: Hereford Station and lines are operational.

A general view of **HEREFORD MPD** on April 13th, 1957. The presence of ex-LNWR 0–8–0 No. 49422 reveals the depots role as the only servicing point within the area, following the pre-BR closure of the ex-LNWR shed at Barrs Court.

Bill Potter

85C(s) LEOMINSTER

Location: East of the line, north of Leominster Station. (OS Map Ref: SO502592)

Directions: Entrance to the shed is effected from the southbound platform.

Closed: April 2nd, 1962.

Description: A brick built 2TS through road shed.

Post Closure History: *Demolished. Most of shed site is occupied by a horses field. (1989)*

The shed yard at **LEOMINSTER MPD** appeared to be in danger of disappearing under grass and weeds when viewed on July 5th, 1959. *WT Stubbs*

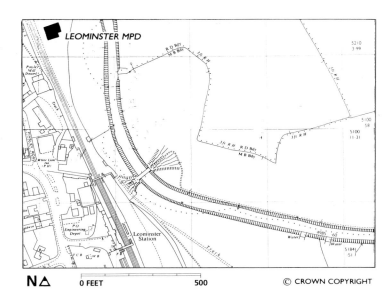

N△ 0 FEET 500 © CROWN COPYRIGHT

Map Dated: 1968 (Shed Superimposed)

Site Location: East of the town centre, on the east side of Worcester Road (A44)

Track Status: Leominster Station and line are operational

85C(s) ROSS ON WYE

Location; The shed is west of the line, south of Ross on Wye Station. (OS Map Ref;SO609243)

Directions; Entrance to the shed is effected from the station platform.

Closed; October 1963.

Description; A stone built 1TS dead ended shed.

Post Closure History; *Still Standing (1989)*

Ex-GWR 5700 Class 0–6–0PT No. 4657 stands outside of **ROSS ON WYE MPD** on a June day in 1957. *Bill Potter*

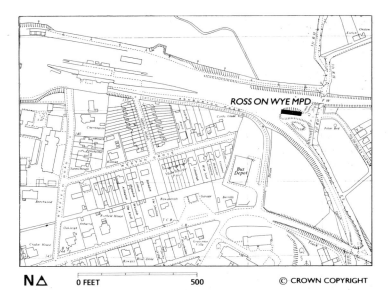

N△ 0 FEET 500 © CROWN COPYRIGHT

Map Dated: 1968

Site Location: West of the town centre, north of Gloucester Road (A40)

Track Status: Ross on Wye Station closed in 1964. Lines lifted.

85C(s) KINGTON

Location: North of the line, west of Kington Station. (OS Map Ref: SO302570)

Directions: Entrance to the shed is effected from the station platform.

Closed: February 1951.

Description: A brick built ITS through road shed.

Post Closure History: *Demolished. The former track bed is now occupied by the A44 bypass and the shed site is part of a horses paddock. (1989)*

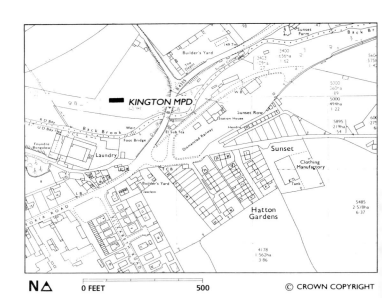

N△   0 FEET   500   © CROWN COPYRIGHT

Map Dated: 1974 (Shed Superimposed)

Site Location: In the east of the town, on the west side of the B4355.

Track Status: Kington Station closed in 1955. Lines lifted

KINGTON MPD brings a touch of industrial landscape to its otherwise rural surroundings in this view from the adjacent roadway.   *Bernard Matthews Collection*

85C(s) LEDBURY

Location: Adjacent to the north side of Ledbury Station.(OS Map Ref: SO709386)

Directions: Entrance to the shed is effected from the station platform.

Closed: July 1964.

Description: Consisting of an engine pit, turntable and coaling platform. There were no shed buildings.

Post Closure History: *Lines lifted. (1970)*

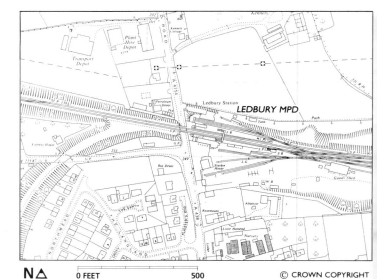

N△   0 FEET   500   © CROWN COPYRIGHT

Map Dated: 1967

Site Location: North of the town centre, on the east side of the A4154.

Track Status: Ledbury Station and line are operational.

Ex-GWR Class 4200 2–8–0T No. 5243 takes time off from banking duties as it simmers alongside the small coaling stage at **LEDBURY MPD** on July 11th, 1959.

Bill Potter

86G(s) PONTRILAS

Location: West of the Pontrilas to Hay line, north of Pontrilas Station. (OS Map Ref: SO399282)

Directions: Leave the station by the approach road, cross the A40 and proceed along the B4347. Pass through Ewyass Harold, bear first right along an unclassified road and after a short distance the Hay branch crosses this road on the level. The shed is on the right hand side of the line about 600 yards south of this level crossing.

Closed: February 2nd, 1953.

Description: A wooden built 1TS through road shed.

Post Closure History: *Demolished. The branch line is now in use as a farm track and the shed site is part of a large field. (1989)*

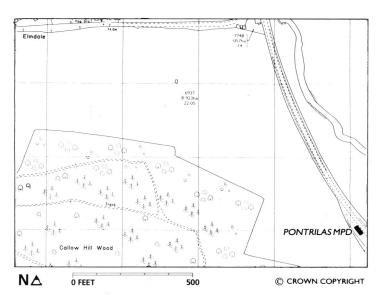

The remote and little-photographed shed at **PONTRILAS MPD**
Allan Sommerfield Collection

Map Dated: 1976 (Shed Superimposed)
Site Location: About a half mile north of Pontrilas.
Track Status: Pontrilas Station closed in 1958. Main line operational. Hay branch lines lifted.

PONTRILAS MPD in 1989, its brief flirtation with the Industrial Revolution over, this portion of the Hay Branch and the shed site returns to a rustic role as a track linking two fields.
Paul Smith

WEST MIDLANDS

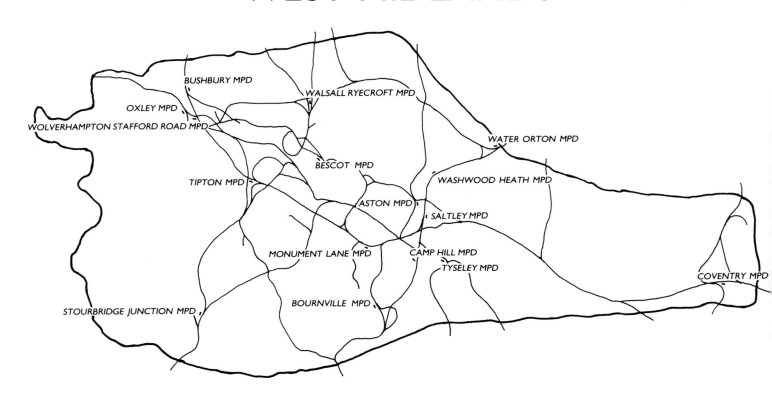

2D COVENTRY

Location: In the fork of the Rugby and Warwick lines, east of Coventry Station. (OS Map Ref: SP335781)

Directions: Turn right out of the station into Park Road and right again into Quinton Road. The shed entrance is on the right hand side just past the railway bridge.

Closed: November 17th, 1958.

Description: A brick built 4TS dead ended shed

Post Closure History: Used as a store for withdrawn locomotives after closure, but subsequently demolished and is now the site of Coventry Power Signal Box. (1989)

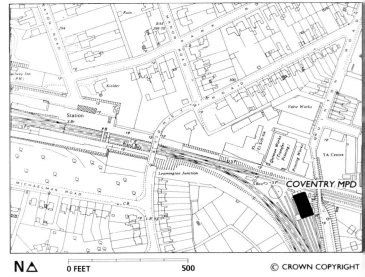

N△   0 FEET   500   © CROWN COPYRIGHT

Map Dated: 1951
Site Location: South of the city centre, east of Warwick Road (A46)
Track Status: Coventry Station and lines are operational.

Ex-LMS 0–8–0 No. 49441 stands in the yard of **COVENTRY MPD** on December 19th, 1957. Despite the 'new' look of the shed it had less than a year to go before closure and eventual obliteration as part of Coventry Power Signal Box site.

Ken Fairey

3A BESCOT

Location: At the north end of Bescot Station, on the west side of the line. (OS Map Ref: SP005962)

Directions: Entrance to the shed is effected from the station platform.

Closed: March 28th, 1966.

Description: A brick built 8TS dead ended shed.

Post Closure History: *Still Standing, in use for wagon repairs. A purpose built diesel depot (Code BS) has been built in the shed yard. (1989).*

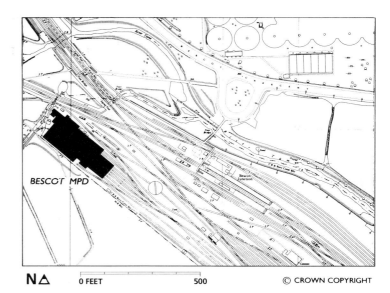

N△　　0 FEET　　　　　　500　　　　© CROWN COPYRIGHT

Map Dated: 1963
Site Location: On the south side of Walsall, immediately west of the M6.
Track Status: Bescot Station and lines are operational.

A side view of **BESCOT MPD** taken on June 11th, 1949. The scene is much changed today with the shed building surrounded by overhead power lines, the sylvan background engulfed by a housing estate and the photographers vantage point buried under the M6.　　　　　　　　　　*John Edgington*

3B BUSHBURY

Location: On the east side of the Stafford line, 1.5 miles north of Wolverhampton High Level Station. (OS Map Ref: SJ917015)

Directions: Go straight ahead outside the station and proceed towards the town centre along Lichfield Street. Turn right into Princes Square and continue along Stafford Street, Lower Stafford Street and eventually Stafford Road. Turn right into Bushbury Lane and the shed entrance is a gate on the left hand side, just past the railway bridge.

Closed: April 10th, 1965.

Description: A brick built 8TS dead ended shed

Post Closure History: *Demolished, the site lay unused for some years but was later redeveloped as a supermarket. (1985)*

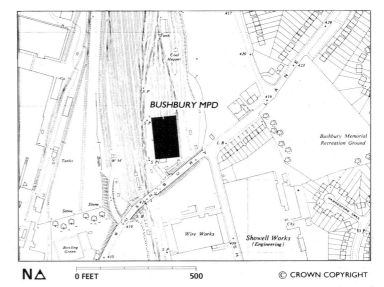

N△　　0 FEET　　　　　　500　　　　© CROWN COPYRIGHT

Map Dated: 1944
Site Location: North of Wolverhampton town centre, east of the A449.
Track Status: Line operational.

A typical ex-LMS shed scene, **BUSHBURY MPD** on April 22nd, 1962.
　　　　　　　　　　WT Stubbs Collection

3C WALSALL RYECROFT

Location: In the fork of the Walsall to Lichfield and Cannock lines, north of Walsall Station. (OS Map Ref: SP015998)

Directions: Turn right outside of the station along Park Street, left into Darwell Street and proceed along Hatherton Street. Turn right at the end, fork left into Cecil Street, turn left into Mill Lane and the shed entrance is on the left hand side just past the railway bridge.

Closed: June 9th, 1958 (Steam)

Description: A brick built 12TS dead ended shed.

Post Closure History: *Used as a dmu depot until the mid sixties, when it was totally closed. Now demolished.*

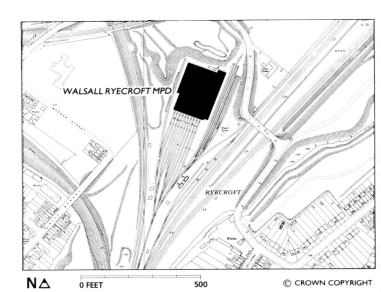

Map Dated: 1963
Site Location: North of the town centre, east of the A34.
Track Status: Lines operational.

After closure **WALSALL RYECROFT MPD** found employment as a dmu depot as this view, taken on October 7th, 1962, shows.   *WT Stubbs Collection*

3D ASTON

Location: In the fork of the Aston to Stechford and Aston to Birmingham New Street lines. (OS Map Ref:SP090892)

Directions: Cross the Lichfield Road outside of Aston Station and proceed up Holborn Hill, turning right into Long Acre at the top of the road. The shed entrance is a gate in the wall on the right hand side of the road.

Closed: October 11th, 1965.

Description: A brick built 12TS dead ended shed.

Post Closure History: *Demolished. The whole site has been redeveloped as a commercial vehicle depot for Bristol Street Motors Ltd. (1989)*

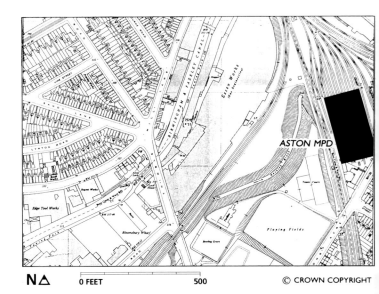

Map Dated: 1952
Site Location: North east of Birmingham city centre, on the east side of Lichfield Road.
Track Status: Aston Station and lines are operational.

ASTON MPD on May 4th, 1958.   *Allan Sommerfield Collection*

3E MONUMENT LANE

Location: The shed is on the south side of the Birmingham New Street to Wolverhampton line, adjacent to the entrance to the tunnel into New Street Station. (OS Map Ref: SP057868)

Directions: Turn right outside of the main entrance to the station, right at the end and proceed along Hill Street. Turn left at the top of the hill, bear right around Paradise Circus and turn left along Broad Street. Turn right into Sheepcote Street, right into St. Vincent Street and the shed entrance is a gate on the right hand side.

Closed: February 12th, 1962.

Description: A brick built 6TS dead ended shed.

Post Closure History: *Used as a Signing-on Point until 1965. Demolished, part of the National Indoor Sports Centre occupies most of the site. (1989)*

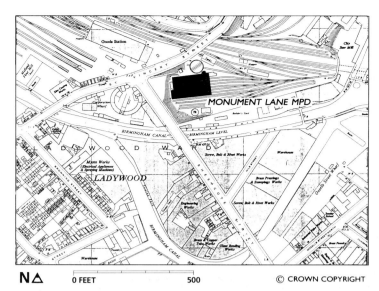

NΔ   0 FEET — 500   © CROWN COPYRIGHT

Map Dated: 1955
Site Location: South west of the city centre, on the west side of Broad Street.
Track Status: Line operational.

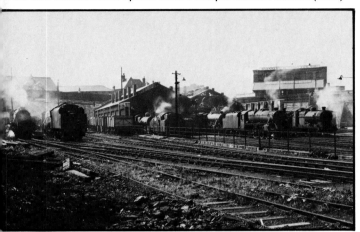

A busy scene at **MONUMENT LANE MPD** photographed in the late 1950s.
Bernard Matthews Collection

3E(s) TIPTON

Location: South of the line, east of Tipton Station. (OS Map Ref: O956924)

Directions: The Goods Yard entrance, on the opposite side of Owen Street to the station, leads to the shed.

Out of Use: 1956.

Description: A brick and wooden built 1TS dead ended shed.

Post Closure History: *Demolished, with one wall remaining, the site is partially occupied by a stanchion carrying pipework across the adjacent canal. (1988)*

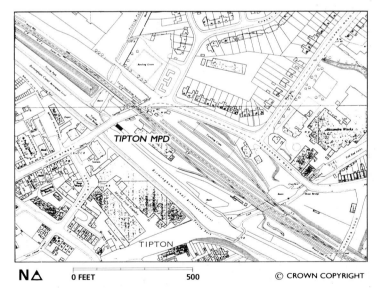

NΔ   0 FEET — 500   © CROWN COPYRIGHT

Map Dated: 1967
Site Location: On the north bank of Birmingham Canal, south of Alexandra Road (B4517)
Track Status: Tipton Station and line are operational

One of the oddest sheds on BR was the tiny structure that formed **TIPTON MPD**. It was sandwiched between two walls, with one wall raised with brickwork and the remainder of the shed built in timber. *Bernard Matthews Collection*

21B BOURNVILLE

Location: On the west side of the line, south of Bournville Station. (OS Map Ref: SP051807)

Directions: Leave the station by the southern exit, cross Mary Vale Road and a gate in the wall leads to a path along the side of the track. This pathway leads to the shed.

Closed: February 15th, 1960.

Description: A brick built roundhouse.

Post Closure History: *Following closure the entire site was rebuilt as a transport depot for Cadbury Brothers Ltd. This itself was demolished in 1988 and replaced by a housing estate.*

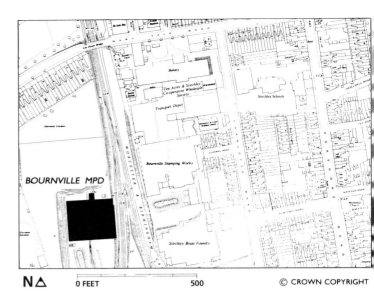

N△   0 FEET   500   © CROWN COPYRIGHT

Map Dated: 1957
Site Location: In the south of Birmingham, west of Pershore Road (A441).
Track Status: Bournville Station and line are operational.

The approaches to **BOURNVILLE MPD** photographed from a passing train on June 1st, 1957.
Bernard Matthews Collection

84A WOLVERHAMPTON STAFFORD ROAD

Location: On the south side of Dunstall Park Station. (OS Map Ref: SJ914002)

Directions: Leave the station by the Stafford Road exit, turn left and the shed entrance is a door in the wall on the left hand side.

Closed: September 9th, 1963.

Description: A brick built 3 roundhouse shed with a corrugated iron 4TS and 3TS dead ended shed built alongside. By BR days the whole shed had become very dilapidated.

Post Closure History: *Demolished, the whole site is now an Industrial Estate. (1989)*

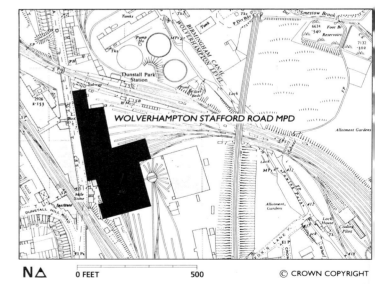

N△   0 FEET   500   © CROWN COPYRIGHT

Map Dated: 1944
Site Location: North of the town centre, on the east side of Dunstall Road (A449)
Track Status: Dunstall Park Station closed in 1968. Lines operational.

Part of the layout of the rambling and semi-derelict buildings which BR inherited and never seemed to have improved at **WOLVERHAMPTON STAFFORD ROAD**, photographed on April 22nd, 1962.
WT Stubbs

21A SALTLEY

Location: East of the line, south of Saltley Station. (OS Map Ref: SP093876)

Directions: From Vauxhall & Duddeston Station: Turn right outside of the station along Duddeston Mill Road and the shed entrance is on the right, just past the railway bridge.

Closed: March 6th, 1967.

Description: A brick built 3 roundhouse building.

Post Closure History: The water tank, offices and side wall of No.2 Roundhouse are still standing, and part of the site is used for car parking. A diesel depot (Code SY) stands in part of the shed yard and the rest of the site is an Industrial Estate (1989).

SALTLEY MPD was always jam packed with freight engines and April 10th, 1949 was no exception when photographed. At this time, with the obvious exception of the massive Beyer-Garratts, the locomotives were, generally, of sufficient size to be easily accomodated within the roundhouses.

The advent of the BR Class 9F 2–10–0s kept a bricklayer and carpenter fully employed in filling in holes in the walls as parking of these somewhat longer locomotives could prove to be tricky. More than one 9F has been known to have sneaked off the depot with its tender half filled with bricks.   *Bernard Matthews Collection*

21A(s) WASHWOOD HEATH

Location: The stabling point is in Washwood Heath Sidings, west of the line, between Saltley and Bromford Bridge Stations. (OS Map Ref: SP112896)

Directions: Access to the sidings is gained from the Industrial Estate sited on the south side of the Tyburn Road (A38), midway between Lichfield Road and the Outer Circle Ring Road (A4040).

Out of Use: February 14th, 1958. *(On this date the last remaining Beyer-Garratt No.47994 was transferred to Crewe Works for scrapping and the stabling point became redundant)*

Description: Consisting of a coaling platform, engine pits, watering facilities, turntable and stabling road. There are no shed buildings.

Post Closure History: Site is part of Washwood Heath Sidings.

The site of **WASHWOOD HEATH MPD** viewed from Bromford Lane Bridge during 1989, with the elevated section of the M6 passing on the right. The stabling road was immediately behind the small bridge in the foreground, the Mess Room was still standing a short distance beyond.   *Paul Smith*

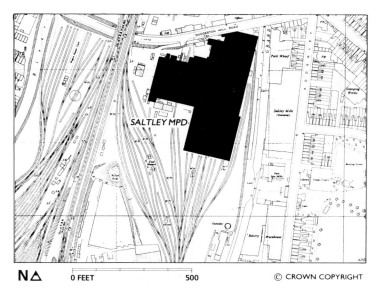

N△   0 FEET   500   © CROWN COPYRIGHT

Map Dated: 1951

Site Location: South east of the city centre, on the west side of Adderley Road (B4145)

Track Status: Lines operational

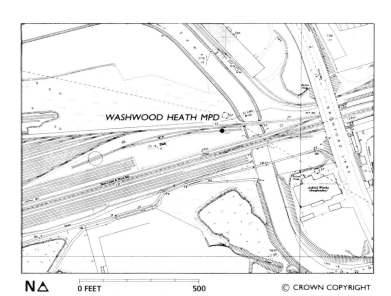

N△   0 FEET   500   © CROWN COPYRIGHT

Map Dated: 1952

Site Location: North east of the city centre, on the west side of Bromford Lane and the River Tame.

Track Status: Lines operational.

Used exclusively for the servicing of Beyer-Garratt locomotives, as these proved to be too cumbersome to handle at Saltley. The stabling point closed completely upon withdrawal of these locomotives, although it was used for a brief period after for Stanier Class 8Fs.

84F STOURBRIDGE JUNCTION

Location: West of the Wolverhampton line, north of Stourbridge Junction Station. (OS Map Ref: SO906849)

Directions: Turn right outside the station, along the approach road, left into Brook Road, right into Red Hill, proceed along Church Road, High Street and continue into Stourbridge Road. Turn right into a rough road, between a level crossing and the Gas Works, bear left up the hill and the shed entrance is on the right hand side.

Closed: July 11th, 1966.

Description: A brick built roundhouse and a brick built 4TS shed with one through road.

Post Closure History: *Demolished. Now site of Housing Estate (1989)*

A small cluster of ex-GW engines occupy an untidy shed yard at **STOURBRIDGE JUNCTION MPD** on June 14th, 1953.   *Allan Sommerfield Collection*

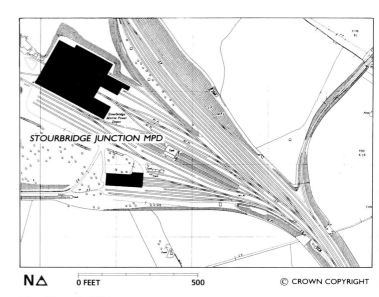

STOURBRIDGE JUNCTION MPD

N△   0 FEET   500   © CROWN COPYRIGHT

Map Dated: 1956
Site Location: In the north of the town, east of the A491.
Track Status: Stourbridge Junction Station and line are operational

21A(s) CAMP HILL

Location: The shed is in Camp Hill Goods Yard on the west side of the Saltley to Kings Norton, Birmingham New Street avoiding line. (OS Map Ref: SP083855)

Directions: From Bordesley Green Station: Turn left at the bottom of the stairs and left again along Camp Hill. Turn right into Stratford Place and the entrance to the Goods Depot is on the left.

Closed: March 6th, 1967 (Steam): 1974 (Totally)

Description: Consisting of an engine pit only, the locomotives stabled within the Goods Shed during week ends.

Post Closure History: *Demolished. The whole site is now buried under an industrial estate and ring road development. (1989)*

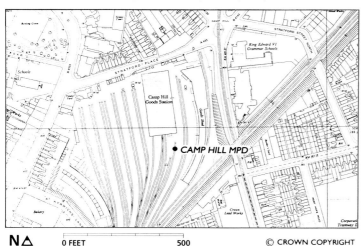

CAMP HILL MPD

N△   0 FEET   500   © CROWN COPYRIGHT

Map Dated: 1952
Site Location: South of Birmingham city centre, west of Stratford Road (A34)
Track Status: Lines operational.

21A(s) WATER ORTON

Location: The shed is within the sidings on the north of the line, west of Water Orton Station. (OS Map Ref: SP170912)

Directions: Entrance to the shed is effected from the station platform.

Closed: March 6th, 1967.

Description: Consisting of two locomotive stand sidings, water tower and engine pits.

Post Closure History: *Track removed. The whole site is now a woodland. (1989)*

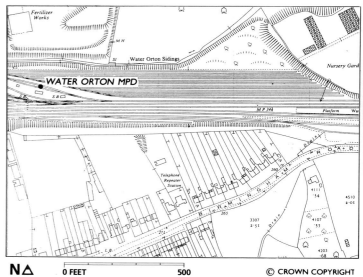

WATER ORTON MPD

N△   0 FEET   500   © CROWN COPYRIGHT

Map Dated: 1954
Site Location: East of Birmingham, on the north side of Birmingham Road (A4118)
Track Status: Water Orton Station and line are operational

84B OXLEY

Location: West of the line, north of Dunstall Park Station. (OS Map Ref: SJ906010)

Directions: Turn right outside of the station, into Stafford Road, cross the canal bridge and turn first left into Jones Road. Turn right into a gateway at the end of this road, adjacent to the viaduct, and a path on the left hand side leads up the embankment to the shed.

Closed: March 6th, 1967.

Description: A brick built double-roundhouse shed.

Post Closure History: *Demolished, now the site of a carriage servicing area. (1988)*

OXLEY MPD as new in 1907.   *Bernard Matthews Collection*

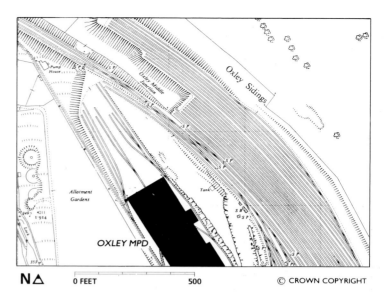

Map Dated: 1944

Site Location: North of town centre, on the west side of the A449

Track Status: Dunstall Park Station closed in 1968. Lines operational.

84E TYSELEY

Location: West of the line, north of Tyseley Station.(OS Map Ref: SP107840)

Directions: Turn right outside of the station, fork right into Wharfedale Road, proceed along Warwick Road and the shed entrance is on the right hand side.

Closed: November 7th, 1966.

Description: A brick built double roundhouse shed.

Post Closure History: *Demolished, the site is occupied by the Birmingham Railway Museum who are in the process of relaying all the floors of the shed and are planning to rebuild it to its original state. (1988)*

TYSELEY MPD was a stereotype GWR roundhouse and this view shows it in its early days in 1916.   *Bernard Matthews Collection*

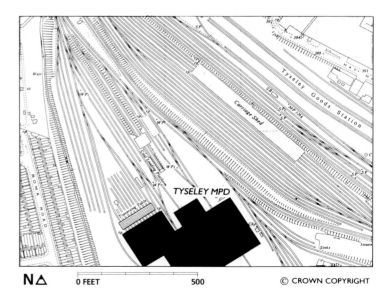

Map Dated: 1951

Site Location: In the south east of the city, adjacent to the north side of Warwick Road (A41)

Track Status: Tyseley Station and line are operational.

NORTHAMPTONSHIRE

15B KETTERING

Location: East of the line, north of Kettering Station. (OS Map Ref: SP864781))

Directions: Go straight ahead outside of the station and the shed entrance is on the left hand side of Station Road.

Closed: June 14th, 1965.

Description: A brick built 4TS dead ended shed.

Post Closure History: Demolished, the site is now a car park. (1989)

Ex-LMS Class 8F 2–8–0 No.48607 simmers in the yard at **KETTERING MPD** on August 25th, 1962. The close proximity of the station platform is clearly visible in this view.
Alec Swain

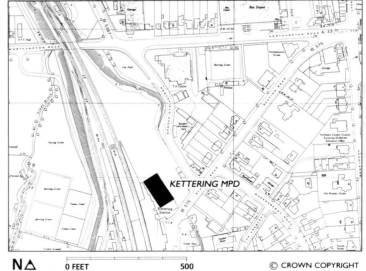

Map Dated: 1968 (Shed Superimposed)

Site Location: In the west of the town, immediately adjacent to the north side of Station Road (B575)

Track Status: Kettering Station and line are operational.

4B NORTHAMPTON

Location: North of the Blisworth to Northampton Bridge Street line.
(OS Map Ref: SP747956)

Directions: Proceed along the approach road out of Northampton Castle Station, turn right into St.Peters Way, right into Bridge Street and continue into Cotton End. Cross the level crossing, by Bridge Street Station, turn right into St.Leonards Road and proceed along Main Road running parallel to the railway line. A footbridge on the right hand side leads to the shed.

Closed: September 27th, 1965.

Description: A brick built 10TS dead ended shed.

Post Closure History: *Demolished*

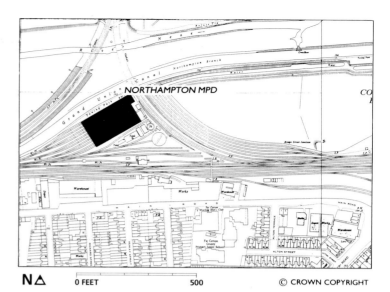

NA △   0 FEET   500   © CROWN COPYRIGHT

Map Dated: 1963

Site Location: South of the town centre, adjacent to the south bank of the Grand Union Canal.

Track Status: Northampton Castle Station and main line is operational. Some other lines lifted.

NORTHAMPTON MPD on July 18th, 1965.   *WT Stubbs Collection*

15A WELLINGBOROUGH

Location: East of the line, north of Wellingborough Midland Road Station.
(OS Map Ref: SP904685)

Directions Turn right outside of the station along a path running parallel to the line,, turn right at the end over Mill Road bridge and the shed entrance is on the left hand sidfe.

Closed: June 13th, 1966.

Description: A complex consisting of 2 brick built roundhouses.

Post Closure History: *No.1 Roundhouse was demolished and replaced by a purpose-built Diesel Depot (Code WO), whilst No.2 Roundhouse became a depot for NCL and is still standing.*

NA △   0 FEET   500   © CROWN COPYRIGHT

Map Dated: 1974 (No.1 Roundhouse Superimposed)

Site Location: In the east of the town, on the east side of Eastfield Road (B573)

Track Status: Wellingborough Station and line are operational.

A busy scene at **WELLINGBOROUGH MPD** on June 6th, 1959.
Bernard Matthews Collection

16B SPITAL BRIDGE

Location: West of the line, north of Peterborough North Station. (OS Map Ref: TL185992)

Directions: Go straight ahead out of the station, turn left into St.Leonards Street, left into Westwood Street and left again into Mayor's Walk. The shed entrance is on the left hand side, just past the railway bridge.

Closed: February 1st, 1960.

Description: A brick built roundhouse shed.

Post Closure History: Demolished. A Power signal box occupies most of the shed site. (1989)

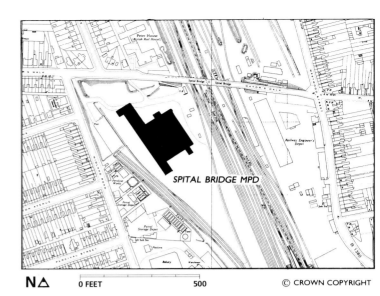

N△   0 FEET   500   © CROWN COPYRIGHT

Map Dated: 1970 (Shed Superimposed)
Site Location: West of the town centre.
Track Status: Peterborough North Station and line are operational.

A general view of **SPITAL BRIDGE** taken in 1958   *Bernard Matthews Collection*

35A NEW ENGLAND

Location: East of the line, about 1.5 miles north of Peterborough North Station. (OS Map Ref: TF007179)

Directions: Cross the station yard, turn left into St.Leonards Street, left into Westwood Street and proceed along Walpole Street for about a mile. A broad cinder path, by the junction with Lincoln Road, on the left hand side leads over a footbridge to the shed.

Closed: September 28th, 1968.

Description: A brick built 9TS through road shed.

Post Closure History: Demolished. Bourges Boulevard occupies part of the shed site.

N△   0 FEET   250   © CROWN COPYRIGHT

Map Dated: 1964
Site Location: On the south side of the A47, north of the city centre.
Track Status: Peterborough North Station and line are operational.

A couple of ex-LNER A4 pacifics grace this view of **NEW ENGLAND MPD**, taken on September 8th, 1963.   *WT Stubbs Collection*

38E WOODFORD HALSE

Location: East of the main line, north of Woodford & Hinton Station. (OS Map Ref: SP543534)

Directions: Turn right out of the station under the bridge and turn left into a cinder path between a block of houses and the line. Proceed along this path, cross the road at the end and another cinder path, opposite, leads to the shed.

Closed: June 14th, 1965.

Description: A brick built 6TS dead ended shed.

Post Closure History: Demolished. Part of the site is occupied by the Great Central Way Industrial Estate, the remainder has been reinstated as agricultural land. (1989)

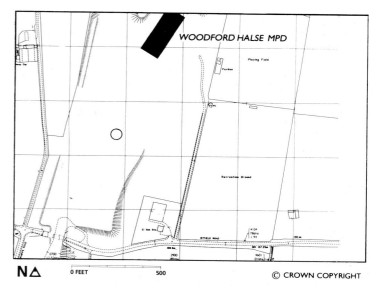

WOODFORD HALSE MPD

N△   0 FEET   500   © CROWN COPYRIGHT

Map Dated: 1979 (Shed Superimposed)

Site Location: North of the town, on the north side of Byfield Road. Woodford Halse is midway between Banbury and Daventry, on the east side of the A361.

Track Status: Woodford & Hinton Station closed in 1966. Lines lifted.

A few locomotives are scattered around **WOODFORD HALSE MPD** on August 21st, 1960.
WT Stubbs Collection

Locomotives in store at **WELLINGBOROUGH MPD** on August 19th, 1959, the Crosti Boilered Class 9Fs awaiting removal to works for conversion to orthodox working, the ex-MR Class 2F 0–6–0 No. 58215 surplus to requirements.
Ken Fairey

PART SEVEN
MONMOUTH & SOUTH WALES

MONMOUTH   SOUTH WALES

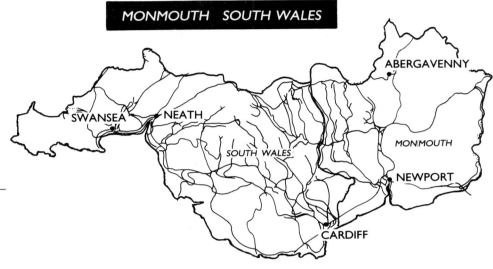

ABERGAVENNY

SWANSEA   NEATH

MONMOUTH

SOUTH WALES

NEWPORT

CARDIFF

BRITISH RAILWAYS

ABERGAVENNY (Sid Nash

MONMOUTH

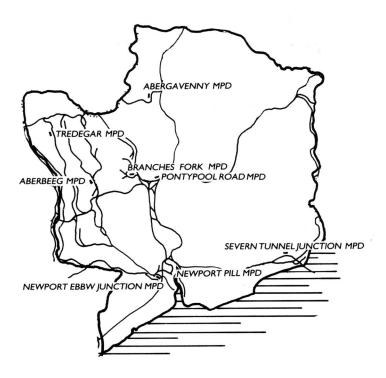

36A NEWPORT EBBW JUNCTION

Location: West of the main line, about 1 mile west of Newport Station. (OS Map Ref: ST300861)

Directions: Cross the station yard, turn right into High Street, fork, left into Commercial Street, right into Cardiff Road and proceed along for about a mile. Pass under a railway bridge and turn left into a drive. This leads to the shed.

Closed: October 1965.

Description: A brick built double roundhouse shed.

Post Closure History: Demolished. Now a housing estate (1987)

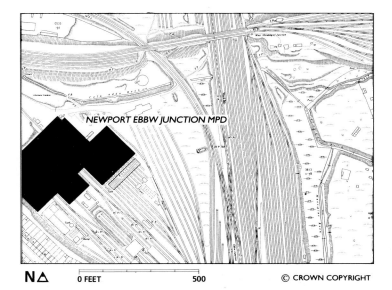

NEWPORT EBBW JUNCTION MPD

N△   0 FEET   500   © CROWN COPYRIGHT

Map Dated: 1957
Site Location: West of the town centre, south of Cardiff Road (A48)
Track Status: Main line operational

EBBW JUNCTION MPD displays part of its enormous collection of shunting locomotives to visiting enthusiasts on June 19th, 1949.   *John Edgington*

86B NEWPORT PILL

Location: In the Newport Docks. (OS Map Ref: ST313862)

Directions: Cross the yard outside of Newport Station, turn right into High Street, fork left into Commercial Road, proceed along Commercial Street and bear right into Alexandra Road. Turn right into Watch Horse Parade and the entrance to the Docks is at the end. The shed entrance is on the right hand side of the Dock Road, just inside the entrance.

Closed: June 17th, 1963.

Description: A brick built 2TS dead ended shed.

Post Closure History: Demolished. The site is occupied by a BRS depot and wood yard. (1987)

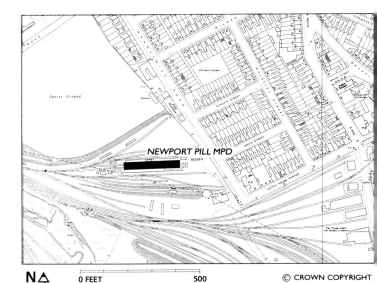

N△   0 FEET   500   © CROWN COPYRIGHT

Map Dated: 1956
Site Location: South of the town centre, on the west bank of the River Usk
Track Status: Lines lifted

Steam locomotion appears to be nearly at an end at **NEWPORT PILL MPD**, with Class 08s well represented, when photographed on September 23rd, 1962. Newport's famous transporter bridge dominates the background.
WT Stubbs Collection

86E SEVERN TUNNEL JUNCTION

Location: North of the junction of the Swindon and Gloucester lines, east of Severn Tunnel Junction Station.(OS Map Ref: ST468876)

Directions: A path runs from the station to the shed along the side of the line.

Closed: October 1965.

Description: A brick built 6TS through road shed.

Post Closure History: Used for motor vehicle storage for some years, but subsequently demolished.

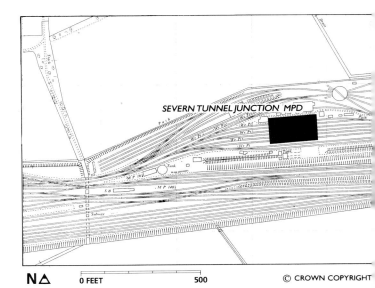

N△   0 FEET   500   © CROWN COPYRIGHT

Map Dated: 1965
Site Location: About 6 miles west of Chepstow, on the south side of the B4245.
Track Status: Severn Tunnel Junction Station and line are operational

SEVERN TUNNEL JUNCTION MPD on September 13th, 1953. *Bill Potter*

36G PONTYPOOL ROAD

Location: West of the Newport line, near the junction of the Aberdare line, south of Pontypool Road Station. (OS Map Ref: ST295997)
Directions: Turn right outside of the station along the approach road, cross the main road and proceed along a drive leading down a steep slope. This leads to a cinder path running parallel to the line and a boarded crossing leads from the right hand side to the shed.
Closed: May 1965
Description: A brick built roundhouse adjoining an 8TS shed with one through road passing through both buildings.
Post Closure History: Demolished

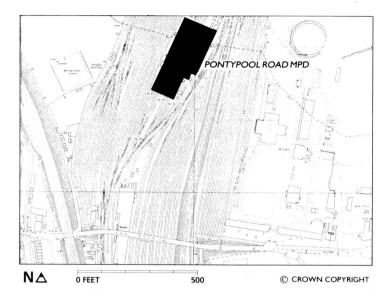

PONTYPOOL ROAD MPD

N △   0 FEET   500   © CROWN COPYRIGHT

Map Dated: 1965
Site Location: East of Pontypool on the north side of New Road.
Track Status: Pontypool (Road) Station and line are operational

A fine mixture of locomotives were on view at **PONTYPOOL ROAD MPD** when photographed on October 14th, 1962. *Bill Potter*

36G(s) BRANCHES FORK

Location: On the north side of the line from Pontnewynydd Junction to Cwmnantddu and Cwmffrwdoer Colliery Branches, east of Branches Fork Junction. (OS Map Ref: SO268016)
Directions: From the junction of Hanbury Road and the Pontypool to Blaenavon Road (A4043) at Pontnewynydd; Follow the Hanbury Road in a westerly direction and turn left along a track, just past Albion Place. Follow the path around to the right and almost immediately turn left along another pathway. Cross the footbridge over a small stream and turn right up the bank. This pathway leads along the side of the line to the shed.
Closed: October 20th, 1951
Description: A brick built 1TS dead ended shed.
Post Closure History: Demolished

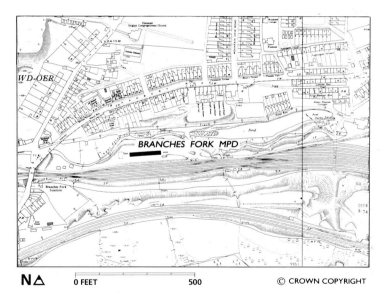

WD-OER

BRANCHES FORK MPD

N △   0 FEET   500   © CROWN COPYRIGHT

Map Dated: 1962
Site Location: North west of Pontypool, west of the A4043.
Track Status: Some lines lifted.

The somewhat obscure **BRANCHES FORK MPD**, with all track removed but otherwise basically intact on June 15th, 1953. *WT Stubbs Collection*

86H ABERBEEG

Location: On the west side of the goods line between Aberbeeg and Llanhilleth Stations. (OS Map Ref: SO210110)

Directions: A narrow road leads down the steep hill to Glandwr at the bottom of the valley from the west side of the main Aberbeeg to Llanhilleth Road (A467), about midway between the two towns. A path leads to the shed from the left hand side of this narrow road, just past the railway bridge.

Closed: December 1964.

Description: A brick built 4TS dead ended shed.

***Post Closure History**: Still Standing. In industrial use by Bawn Brassfounders. (1987)*

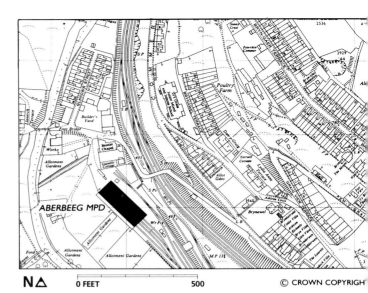

The yard and shed buildings at **ABERBEEG MPD** on October 14th, 1962.
Bill Potter

Map Dated: 1962
Site Location: On west side of the A497.
Track Status: Lines operational.

86K ABERGAVENNY

Location: On the west side of the LNWR line, south of Abergavenny (Brecon Road) Station. (OS Map Ref: SO291142)

Directions: Turn left outside the station into Brecon Road, right into St.Helen's Road and right again at the end into Union Road. The shed entrance is just past the railway bridge on the left hand side.

Closed: January 6th, 1958. *(Classed as a Stabling Point only from November 22nd, 1954)*

Description: A stone built 12TS dead ended shed, latterly the shed had been reduced to 6 tracks.

***Post Closure History**: Demolished. Site Unused.(1972)*

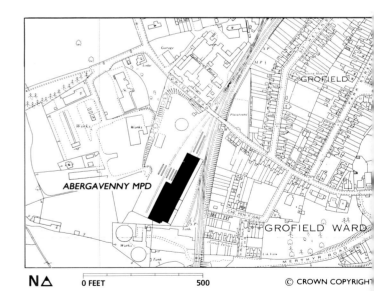

A derelict **ABERGAVENNY MPD** on September 25th, 1962.
WT Stubbs Collection

Map Dated: 1965
Site Location: In the south west of the town, on the west side of the Merthyr Road (A465).
Track Status: Abergavenny Station and line are operational.

6K(s) TREDEGAR

Location: The shed is west of the line, at the south end of Tredegar Station. (OS Map Ref: SO145083)
Directions: The shed entrance is a gate in the Station Yard.
Closed: June 11th, 1960.
Description: A brick built 4TS dead ended shed.
Post Closure History: *Still standing in a derelict condition as late as 1975.*

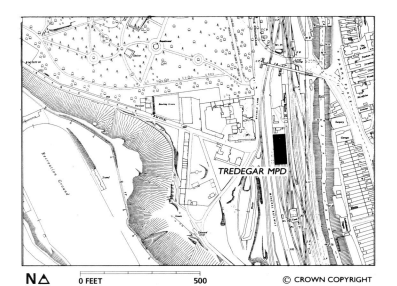

N△   0 FEET   500   © CROWN COPYRIGHT

Map Dated: 1961
Site Location: In the centre of the town, on the west bank of Sirhywi River.
Track Status: Tredegar Station closed in 1960. Lines lifted.

TREDEGAR MPD and station site lingered on in a semi-derelict state for many years after closure and removal of track. This view was taken on September 24th, 1962 and was little changed right up until at least the mid-70s. *WT Stubbs Collection*

Interior view of the cramped conditions at **FERNDALE MPD** on August 30th, 1964, with some of its 5600 Class 0–6–2T locomotives all coaled up and awaiting their next turn of duty.
Ken Fairey

SOUTH WALES

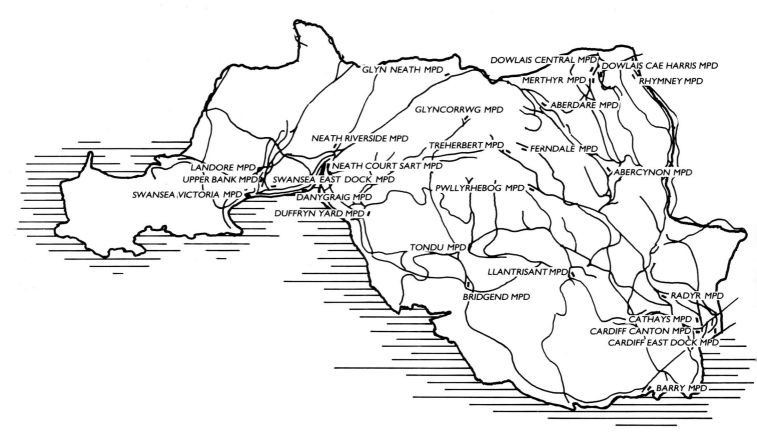

GLYN NEATH MPD

DOWLAIS CENTRAL MPD
DOWLAIS CAE HARRIS MPD
MERTHYR MPD
RHYMNEY MPD
ABERDARE MPD

GLYNCORRWG MPD

NEATH RIVERSIDE MPD
TREHERBERT MPD
FERNDALE MPD

LANDORE MPD
NEATH COURT SART MPD
ABERCYNON MPD
UPPER BANK MPD
SWANSEA EAST DOCK MPD
SWANSEA VICTORIA MPD
PWLLYRHEBOG MPD
DANYGRAIG MPD
DUFFRYN YARD MPD

TONDU MPD

LLANTRISANT MPD
RADYR MPD

BRIDGEND MPD
CATHAYS MPD
CARDIFF CANTON MPD
CARDIFF EAST DOCK MPD

BARRY MPD

86C CARDIFF CANTON

Location: On the south side of the main line, west of Cardiff General Station. (OS Map Ref: ST171759)

Directions: Turn left outside Cardiff General Station, along the side of Central Square and turn left again by Wales Empire Pool into Wood Street and cross the river. Continue along Tudor Street, Ninian Park Road and turn left into DeCroche Place, about 200 yards past the junction of Clare Road. A footbridge leads to the shed from the end of this cul-de-sac.

Closed: September 10th, 1962 (Steam).

Description: A brick built structure composed of a 28 stall roundhouse and a 6TS dead ended shed.

Post Closure History: *The roundhouse has been demolished and the whole site has been rebuilt as a Diesel Depot (Code CF).*

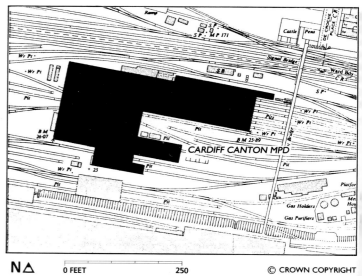

CARDIFF CANTON MPD

N△   0 FEET   250   © CROWN COPYRIGHT

Map Dated: 1954
Site Location: West of the city centre, south of Ninian Park Road (A4055)
Track Status: Lines operational.

A general view of the large depot at **CARDIFF CANTON MPD** with a fine assortment of ex-GWR locomotives in the yard on September 13th, 1953.

Bill Potter

86D LLANTRISANT

Location: North of the junction of the main and Coed Ely lines, west of Llantrisant Station. (OS Map Ref: ST033819)

Directions: Turn left outside of the station into the approach road, continue through the gate at the end into the Goods Yard and follow the railway track. This leads to the shed.

Closed: October 1964.

Description: A stone built 3TS through road shed.

Post Closure History: Demolished

LLANTRISANT MPD on April 23rd, 1950.   *Bill Potter*

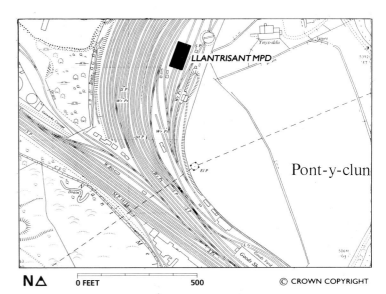

Map Dated: 1961

Site Location: South west of the town at Pont-y-clun. On the west side of the A4222.

Track Status: Llantrisant Station closed in 1964. Main line operational.

86F TONDU

Location: In the fork of the Ogmore Valley and Maesteg lines, at the north end of Tondu Station. (OS Map Ref: SS895846)

Directions: A boarded crossing leads to the shed from the station platforms.

Closed: February 1964.

Description: A brick built roundhouse shed.

Post Closure History: Demolished. Site Unused.

The compact roundhouse at **TONDU MPD** photographed on September 22nd, 1962.   *WT Stubbs Collection*

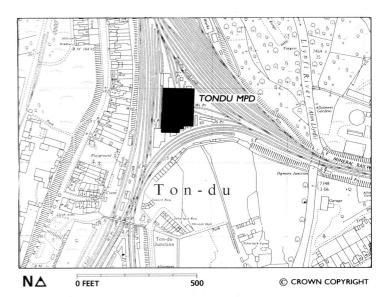

Map Dated: 1964

Site Location: South east of the town, east of Maesteg Road (A4063)

Track Status: Tondu Station closed in 1970. Some lines operational.

86F(s) BRIDGEND

Location: On the east side of the line, north of Bridgend Station. (OS Map Ref: SS905805)

Directions: A drive off the left hand side of Coity Road (A4061), north of the railway bridge, leads to the shed.

Closed: April 1950.

Description: A stone built 1TS dead ended shed.

Post Closure History: *Demolished. Now site of Factory.*

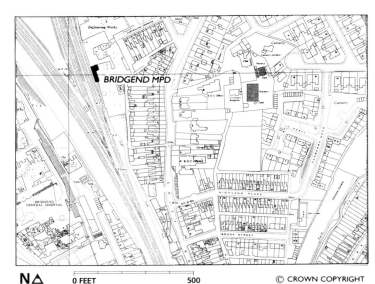

BRIDGEND MPD   *Allan Sommerfield Collection*

Map Dated: 1971 (Shed Superimposed)

Site Location: In the north of the town, on the west side of Coity Road (A4061).

Track Status: Bridgend Station and line are operational

86J ABERDARE

Location: North of the line, west of Aberdare High Level Station. (OS Map Ref: SO002032)

Directions: Turn right outside of Aberdare Low Level Station into Duke Street, and right into Commercial Street. Cross the level crossing and proceed under the railway bridge, turn left into the Goods Yard at the end of Abernant Road and a cinder path leads to the shed.

Closed: March 1st, 1965.

Description: A brick built roundhouse.

Post Closure History: *Demolished*

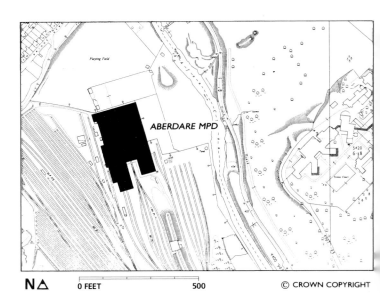

5600 Class 0–6–2T engines Nos. 6622 and 5625 standing on the coaling stage road at **ABERDARE MPD** on October 14th, 1962.   *Bill Potter*

Map Dated: 1962

Site Location: In the east of the town, on the west bank of the Afon Cynon.

Track Status: Aberdare Low Level Station closed in 1964. Lines lifted.

87A NEATH COURT SART

Location: West of the main line, about 1 mile south of Neath General Station. (OS Map Ref: SS740957)

Directions: Turn right outside of the station into Windsor Road, bear right into Briton Ferry Road and continue along for about a mile. Turn right into Collins Street, cross the footbridge and a cinder path leads to the shed.

Closed: June 1965.

Description: A stone built double-roundhouse shed.

Post Closure History: Demolished

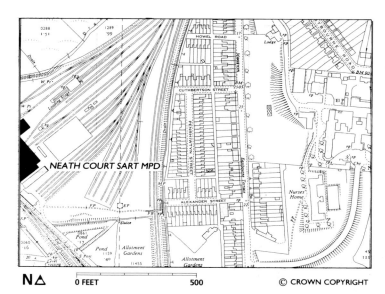

Map Dated: 1952
Site Location: In the west of the town, on the west side of the A48
Track Status: Line operational

A massive depot with barely a locomotive in sight. A pre-war shot of **NEATH COURT SART MPD**   *Allan Sommerfield Collection*

87A(s) GLYN NEATH

Location: On the north side of the line, east of Glyn Neath Station. (OS Map Ref: SN869056)

Directions: Entrance to the shed is effected from the station platform.

Closed: October 5th, 1964.

Description: A brick built 1TS dead ended shed.

Post Closure History: Demolished. Part of the trackbed is buried under a bypass road.

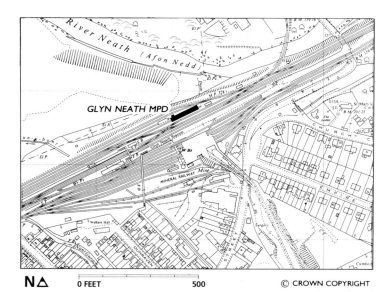

Map Dated: 1962
Site Location: In the south of the town, south of the River Neath
Track Status: Glyn Neath Station closed in 1964. Lines lifted.

The water tank straddles the shed entrance at **GLYN NEATH MPD** as an unidentified 0–6–2T locomotive receives fuel from a wagon parked on the slightly elevated coaling stage.   *Bernard Matthews Collection*

87A(s) NEATH RIVERSIDE

Location: West of the Brecon line, north of Neath Riverside Station. (OS Map Ref: SS752982)

Directions: Turn left outside of Neath General Station into Station Square, proceed along The Parade, turn left into Croft Road and continue into Bridge Street. Turn right at the end into Cadoxton Road and a drive leads to the shed from the right hand side, just past the bridge.

Closed: June 1964.

Description: A brick built 2TS dead ended shed.

Post Closure History: *Still Standing. (1985)*

The modern construction of **NEATH N&B MPD** is clearly visible in this view, taken on April 4th, 1959.
Alec Swain

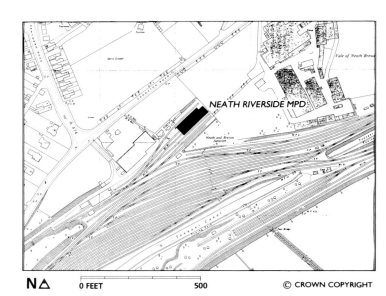

NA   0 FEET   500   © CROWN COPYRIGHT

Map Dated: 1968

Site Location: In the north west of the town, on the south side of Cadoxton Road (A465)

Track Status: Neath Riverside Station closed in 1964. Line operational

Neath Riverside MPD was also known as Neath N&B

87B DUFFRYN YARD

Location: On the east side of the Port Talbot to Maesteg line. (OS Map Ref: SS778896)

Directions: Turn right outside Port Talbot General Station along Talbot Road, turn left into Duffryn Road (by The Talbot Arms Hotel) and the shed entrance is on the left hand side of the road, about 850 yards past the junction of Field Terrace.

Closed: March 2nd, 1964.

Description: A brick built 6TS dead ended shed, latterly only 5 tracks were in use.

Post Closure History: *Demolished*

An elevated view of **DUFFRYN YARD MPD** taken on September 22nd, 1962.
WT Stubbs Collection

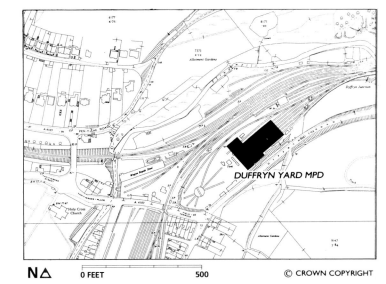

NA   0 FEET   500   © CROWN COPYRIGHT

Map Dated: 1953

Site Location: In the north east of the town, on the north side of the A4107.

Track Status: Lines lifted.

87B(s) GLYNCORRWG

Location: East of Glyncorrwg Station, north of the line. (OS Map Ref: SS876993)

Directions: Access to the shed is gained from the level crossing at the east end of the station.

Closed: June 1965.

Description: A brick and stone built 1TS dead ended shed.

Post Closure History: *Demolished*

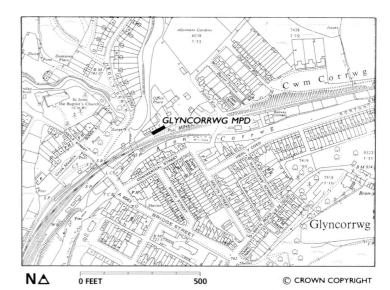

NΔ 0 FEET   500   © CROWN COPYRIGHT

Map Dated: 1962

Site Location: In the north of the town, on the north bank of the Afon Corrwg.

Track Status: Glyncorrwg Station closed in 1930. Lines lifted.

The former South Wales Mineral Railway shed, **GLYNCORRWG MPD** in June 1936. Although closed in GWR days it lasted as a Stabling Point until the end of steam locomotion in the valley.   *Allan Sommerfield Collection*

87C DANYGRAIG

Location: On the south side of the R&SB line, west of Jersey Marine Station. (OS Map Ref: SS694932)

Directions: Turn left outside of Swansea High Street Station along High Street and continue into Castle Street and Wind Street. Turn left into Quay Parade, cross the river bridge and continue into Fabian Street. Pass the entrance to SWANSEA EAST DOCK shed and proceed along Port Tennant Road and then Vale of Neath Road for about 2 miles. Cross the long railway bridge, bear left into the former main road and left again into a Private Road leading to Kings Dock Steel Works. The shed entrance is on the left hand side a short distance along.

Closed: January 4th 1960 (Steam), March 1964 (Totally).

Description: A stone built 4TS shed with 2 through roads, attached to a loco repair and C&W repair building

Post Closure History: *Still Standing. In industrial use by 'Gower Chemicals' (1988)*

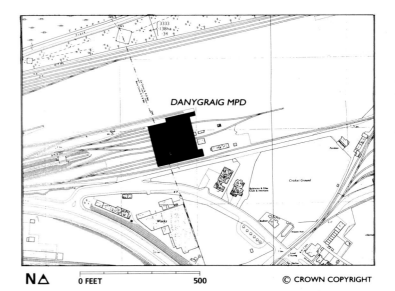

NΔ 0 FEET   500   © CROWN COPYRIGHT

Map Dated: 1971

Site Location: On the west side of Swansea, on the north side of the A483.

Track Status: Lines operational

DANYGRAIG MPD parades some of its famous collection of shunting engines on July 22nd, 1956.   *Ken Fairey*

87D SWANSEA EAST DOCK

Location: North of the line, east of Swansea East Dock Station. (OS Map Ref: SS670931)
Directions: For directions see under DANYGRAIG SHED.
Closed: June 1964.
Description: A brick built 3TS dead ended shed.
Post Closure History: *Demolished*

0–6–0PT locomotives dominate this view of **SWANSEA EAST DOCK MPD** on July 9th, 1950.
John Edgington

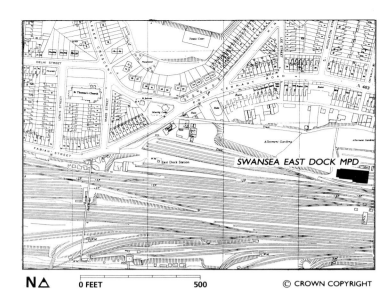

N△   0 FEET   500   © CROWN COPYRIGHT

Map Dated: 1957
Site Location: South east of the city centre, on the south side of Port Tennant Road (A483)
Track Status: Line lifted.

87E LANDORE

Location: In the fork of the Swansea and Cockett lines, north of Swansea High St. Station. (OS Map Ref: SS658952)
Directions: Turn right outside of the station along High Street, fork right into Prince of Wales Road and proceed along Neath Road. A drive on the left hand side between two bridges leads to the shed.
Closed: June 12th, 1961.
Description: Comprising two brick built 4TS sheds, one of which is dead ended.
Post Closure History: *The buildings were demolished and replaced by a purpose-built diesel depot (Code LE).*

An ex-GWR Railcar receives attention amongst a fine collection of steam locomotives at **LANDORE MPD** on May 4th, 1952.
Bill Potter

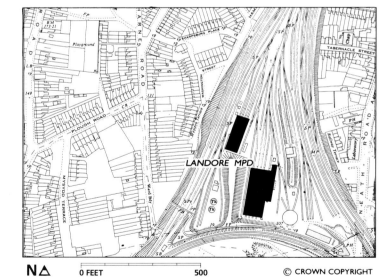

N△   0 FEET   500   © CROWN COPYRIGHT

Map Dated: 1951
Site Location: North of the city centre, adjacent to the west side of Neath Road (A4067)
Track Status: Lines operational.

87K SWANSEA VICTORIA

Location: South of the ex-LMS line between Swansea Bay and Swansea (Victoria) Stations. (OS Map Ref: SS653923)

Directions: Turn left outside of Swansea (Victoria) Station along Victoria Road, proceed along Oystermouth Road, turn left into Paxton Street and the shed entrance is on the right hand side, just past the railway bridge.

Closed: March 2nd, 1959.

Description: A brick built 6TS dead ended shed.

Post Closure History: Demolished

SWANSEA VICTORIA MPD looked decidedly on its last legs when photographed in 1959, the year of closure.   *Alec Swain*

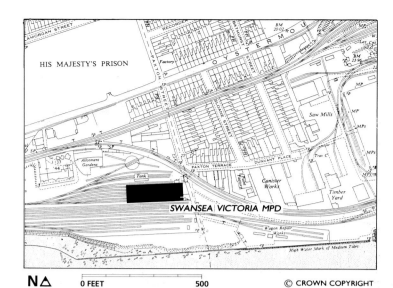

Map Dated: 1951

Site Location: In the south of the city, on the south side of Oystermouth Road (B4290)

Track Status: Lines lifted.

87K(s) UPPER BANK

Location: West of the line, north of Upper Bank Station. (OS Map Ref: SS669955)

Directions: There is a path from the station to the shed.

Closed: February 4th, 1963

Description: A stone built 2TS shed with 1 through road.

Post Closure History: Demolished

A distant view of **UPPER BANK MPD** on September 15th, 1962.   *Alec Swain*

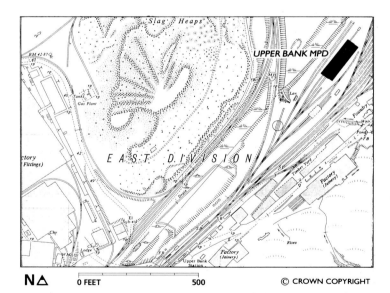

Map Dated: 1950

Site Location: North east of Swansea, on the north side of the B4292.

Track Status: Upper Bank Station closed in 1950. Lines lifted.

88A CARDIFF CATHAYS

Location: On the west side of the Landaff line about three quarters of a mile north of Cardiff Queen Street Station. (OS Map Ref: ST180775)

Directions: Turn right outside Cardiff General Station into Saunders Road and left into St.Mary's Street, continuing into High Street. Turn right into Duke Street and left almost immediately into Kingsway. Continue into North Road, turn right into Corbett Road and the shed entrance is on the left hand side, just before the railway bridge.

Closed: 1961 (Steam), November 1964 (Totally).

Description: A stone built 9TS dead ended shed.

Post Closure History: Demolished. The entire site is covered by Cardiff University. (1989)

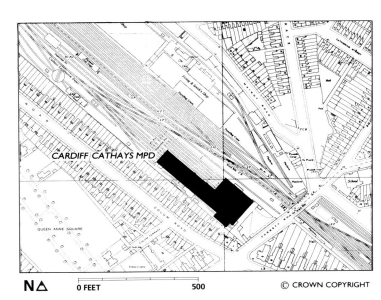

N△   0 FEET   500   © CROWN COPYRIGHT

Map Dated: 1954
Site Location: North of the city centre, east of the A470.
Track Status: Line operational

CARDIFF CATHAYS MPD plays host to a mixed bag collection of tank engines on October 3rd, 1954.
Bill Potter

88A(s) RADYR

Location: West of the Taff Vale main line, between Llandaff and Radyr Stations. (OS Map Ref: ST139798)

Directions: Turn left out of Radyr Station into Junction Terrace and left along a road through the Engineers Yard. This becomes a path which follows the main line and leads to the shed.

Closed: July 26th, 1965.

Description: A brick built 4TS dead ended shed.

Post Closure History: Demolished. Site now occupied by sidings. (1987)

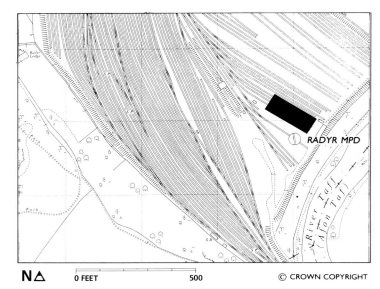

N△   0 FEET   500   © CROWN COPYRIGHT

Map Dated: 1969
Site Location: South east of the town centre, on the east side of Heol Isaf (B4262) and on the west bank of the River Taff
Track Status: Radyr Station and line are operational.

An archetypal ex-GWR scene. **RADYR MPD** was photographed on September 22nd, 1962.
WT Stubbs Collection

88B CARDIFF EAST DOCK

Location: In the heart of Cardiff Dockland. (OS Map Ref: ST197750)

Directions: Turn right outside Cardiff General Station into Saunders Road, cross St.Mary's Street and continue into Customhouse Street. Turn right under the railway bridge into Bute Street and after a short distance, left into Herbert Street. After half a mile turn right into the docks just before a level crossing and the shed entrance is on the left hand side of the Dock Road about three quarters of a mile further along.

Closed: August 2nd, 1965.

Description: A brick built 8TS dead ended shed.

Post Closure History: Demolished

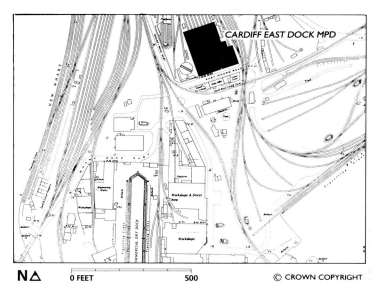

CARDIFF EAST DOCK MPD on September 23rd, 1962, shortly after the transfer *en bloc* of Cardiff Canton's steam locomotive allocation which gave the depot a new lease of life and prolonged its use for another three years.

WT Stubbs Collection

Map Dated: 1954

Site Location: In Cardiff Dockland immediately north of the junction of Junction Lock Road and Tyneside Road.

Track Status: Most lines lifted.

88C BARRY

Location: On the south side of the line, east of Barry Station. (OS Map Ref: ST108672)

Directions: Turn right outside of the station into Broad Street. Turn first right under the railway bridge and a cinder path leads to the shed from the right hand side.

Closed: September 1964.

Description: A brick built 6TS through road shed.

Post Closure History: Still Standing. In use as a Wagon Works. (1987)

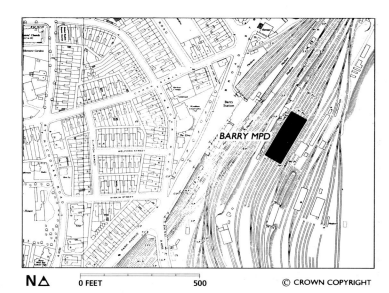

BARRY MPD on September 22nd, 1962.   *WT Stubbs Collection*

Map Dated: 1956

Site Location: In the south west of the town, on the east side of Broad Street (A4055)

Track Status: Barry Station and line are operational.

88D MERTHYR

Location: East of the line, south of Merthyr Station. (OS Map Ref: SO051058)

Directions: Turn right outside of the station across the Station Yard and proceed along a footpath leading into Tramroad Side North. Continue along this road and the shed entrance is on the right hand side.

Closed: November 2nd, 1964.

Description: A brick built 3TS dead ended shed.

Post Closure History: *Still Standing, In industrial use. (1989)*

A post-1948 view of **MERTHYR MPD**.   *Bill Potter*

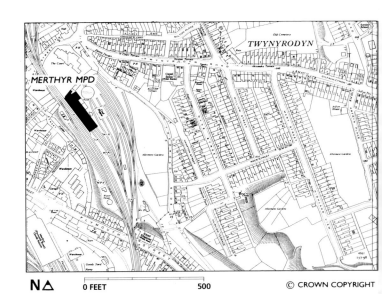

N△   0 FEET   500   © CROWN COPYRIGHT

Map Dated: 1958

Site Location: South of the town centre, on the north side of High Street (A470)

Track Status: Merthyr Station and line are operational.

88D(s) DOWLAIS CAE HARRIS

Location: On the west side of the line, about 150 yards south of Dowlais Cae Harris Station. (OS Map Ref:SO074770)

Directions: Entrance to the shed is effected from the station platform.

Closed: December 1964

Description: A stone built 3TS shed with 1 through road.

Post Closure History: *Demolished*

A strangely deserted **DOWLAIS CAE HARRIS MPD** on July 6th, 1952.
Bill Potter

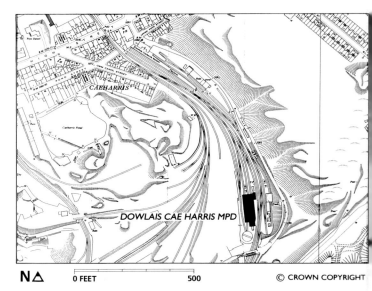

N△   0 FEET   500   © CROWN COPYRIGHT

Map Dated: 1963

Site Location: North east of Merthyr Tydfil, on the south side of the A465.

Track Status: Dowlais Cae Harris Station closed in 1964. Lines lifted.

88D(s) DOWLAIS CENTRAL

Location: West of the line, adjacent to Dowlais Central Station. (OS Map Ref: SO065080)

Directions: Entrance to the shed is effected from the station platform.

Closed: May 1960

Description: A brick built 1TS dead ended shed

Post Closure History: *Demolished*

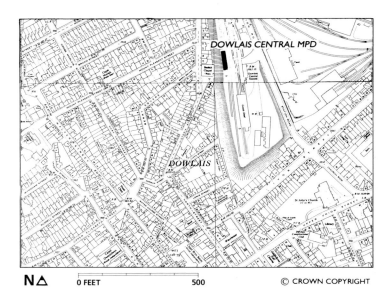

N△   0 FEET   500   © CROWN COPYRIGHT

Map Dated: 1957

Site Location: North east of Merthyr Tydfil, in the north of Dowlais.

Track Status: Dowlais Central Station closed in 1960. Lines lifted

A view very much synonymous with the early days of BR, before the oddments in locomotive stock inherited from the GWR were sifted out. Ex-Taff Vale Railway Class O4 Rebuild 0–6–2T No. 292 stands outside **DOWLAIS CENTRAL MPD** on a wet August 26th, 1951.   *Bill Potter*

88D(s) RHYMNEY

Location: West of the line, at the south end of Rhymney Station. (OS Map Ref: SO111074)

Directions: Entrance to the shed is effected from the station platform.

Closed: March 1965.

Description: A stone built 3TS dead ended shed.

Post Closure History: *Demolished*

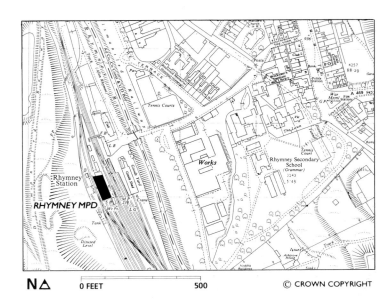

N△   0 FEET   500   © CROWN COPYRIGHT

Map Dated: 1961

Site Location: In the west of the town, on the west bank of the Rhymney River.

Track Status: Rhymney Station and line are operational.

RHYMNEY MPD complete with a typical collection of ex-GWR tank engines on October 14th, 1962.   *Bill Potter*

88E ABERCYNON

Location: On the east side of the line at the north end of Abercynon Station. (OS Map Ref: ST082947)
Directions: The shed and station entrances are adjacent.
Closed: November 2nd, 1964.
Description: A corrugated iron 2TS dead ended shed.
Post Closure History: Still Standing. In use as a Foundry. (1987)

ABERCYNON MPD on October 14th, 1962 with its usual collection of 0–6–0PT and Class 5600 0–6–2T engines.
Bill Potter

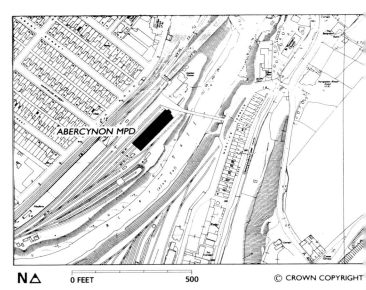

NΔ 0 FEET 500 © CROWN COPYRIGHT

Map Dated: 1960
Site Location: In the south east of the town, on the west bank of the River Taff.
Track Status: Abercynon Station and lines are operational.

88F TREHERBERT

Location: North of the line, east of Treherbert Station. (OS Map Ref: SS940981)
Directions: Go straight ahead out of the station, turn first right, by the Station Hotel, left at the end and first right into Cwmsaerbren Street. The shed entrance is at the end of this street.
Closed: March 1st, 1965.
Description: A corrugated iron 4TS dead ended shed.
Post Closure History: Demolished

A pre-war view of **TREHERBERT MPD** taken in 1931.
Bernard Matthews Collection

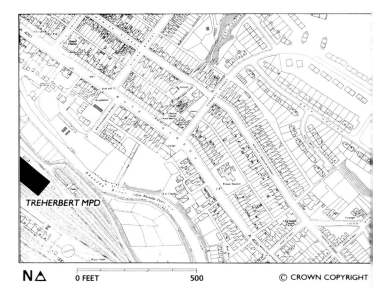

NΔ 0 FEET 500 © CROWN COPYRIGHT

Map Dated: 1962
Site Location: In the south west of the town, west of the Rhondda River and Bute Street (A4061)
Track Status: Treherbert Station and line are operational.

88F(s) FERNDALE

Location: West of the line, north of Ferndale Station.(OS Map Ref: SS996976)

Directions: Turn right outside the station along a street running parallel to the railway. This is a cul-de-sac and a path leads to the shed from a gate at the end of this street.

Closed: September 1964

Description: A stone built 2TS dead ended shed.

Post Closure History: Demolished

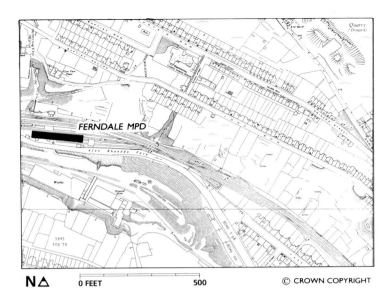

N△   0 FEET   500   © CROWN COPYRIGHT

Map Dated: 1962

Site Location: In the north of the town, on the north bank of the River Rhondda Fach.

Track Status: Ferndale Station closed in 1964. Lines lifted.

FERNDALE MPD on September 24th, 1962.   *WT Stubbs Collection*

88F(s) PWLLYRHEBOG

Location: South of the line at the top of Pwllyrhebog Cable Incline, west of Tonypandy Station. (OS Map Ref: SS986927)

Directions: Turn left outside of the station along Bridge Street, right along Dunraven Street and continue into De Winton Street. Turn left by The Pandy Hotel into Court Street, climb the hill and turn left into a gap between Nos.50 and 51, this leads to an alleyway that runs along the back of the houses and the shed entrance is along this alleyway.

Closed: July 1951.

Description: An asbestos built 1TS dead ended shed.

Post Closure History: Demolished. The whole site, including the incline, is now parkland. (1975)

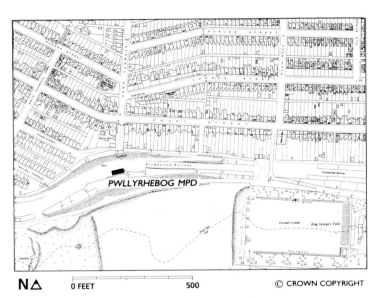

N△   0 FEET   500   © CROWN COPYRIGHT

Map Dated: 1962 (Shed Superimposed)

Site Location: In the west of Tonypandy.

Track Status: All lines lifted.

Taff Vale Railway 0–6–0T No. 195 simmers on the shed road at **PWLLYRHEBOG MPD** on October 14th, 1949.   *Bill Potter*

PART EIGHT

CENTRAL & SOUTH WEST WALES

CARDIGANSHIRE   CARMARTHENSHIRE   MONTGOMERYSHIRE
MERIONETHSHIRE   RADNORSHIRE   PEMBROKESHIRE   BRECKNOCK

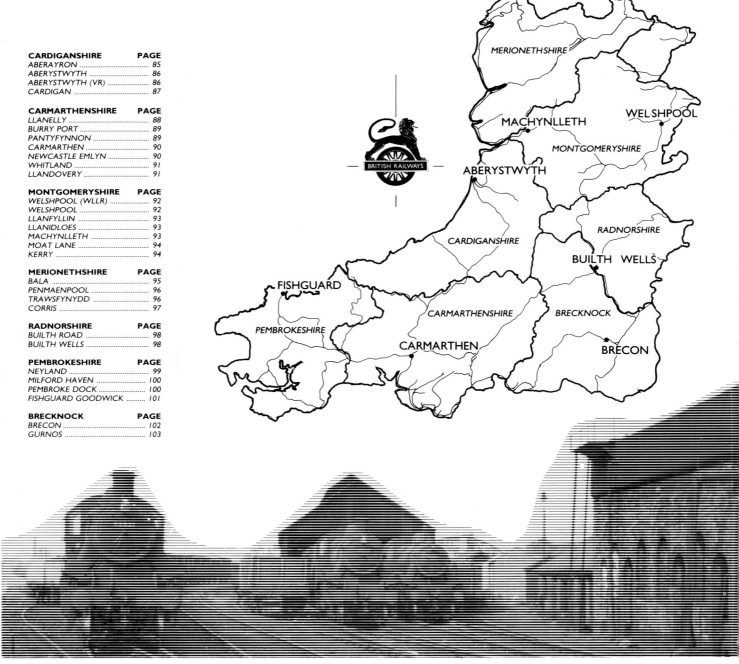

BRECON MPD *(WT Stubbs Collection)*

CARDIGANSHIRE

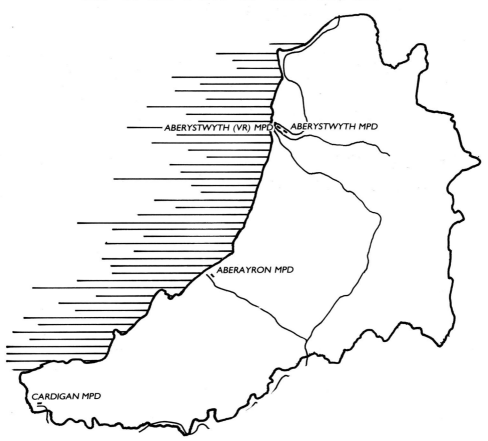

9C(s) ABERAYRON

Location: East of the line, south of Aberayron Station. (OS Map Ref: N462621)

Directions: Entrance to the shed is effected from the station platform.

Closed: April 30th, 1962

Description: A corrugated iron ITS dead ended shed.

Post Closure History: Demolished. Now site of timber merchants. (1989)

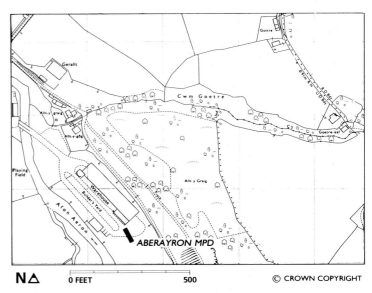

Map Dated: 1973 (Shed Superimposed)
Site Location: In the south of the town, on the east bank of the Afon Aeron.
Track Status: Aberayron Station closed in 1951. Lines lifted.

ABERAYRON MPD photographed shortly after closure on September 19th, 1962.
WT Stubbs Collection

89C(s) ABERYSTWYTH

Location: In the fork of the Machynlleth and Carmarthen lines, east of Aberystwyth Station. (OS Map Ref: SN587813)

Directions: Turn left outside the station into Alexandra Road and left into Park Avenue. A path leads from the end of this road to the shed.

Closed: April 10th, 1965 (Standard gauge steam)

Description: A brick built 2TS through road shed

Post Closure History: Converted for use as the VofR narrow gauge engine shed and still used in that capacity (1989)

9000 Class 0–4–0 No. 9022 simmering in the shed yard at **ABERYSTWYTH MPD** on May 13th, 1953.   *John Edgington*

89C(s) ABERYSTWYTH (VALE OF RHEIDOL)

Location: North of the line, west of Aberystwyth Narrow Gauge Station (OS Map Ref: SN584813)

Directions: The shed entrance is on the right hand side of Park Avenue a short distance before the entrance to ABERYSTWYTH shed.

Out of Use: 1965

Description: A wood and corrugated iron 2TS dead ended shed. The gauge of the lines is 1ft 11.5in.

Post Closure History: Demolished. Site Unused (1972).

The corrugated cladding appears to be well past its best as ex-VR 2–6–2T No. 7 *OWAIN GLYNDWR* takes on water outside the small **ABERYSTWYTH (VR) MPD** on July 29th, 1961.   *Ken Fairey*

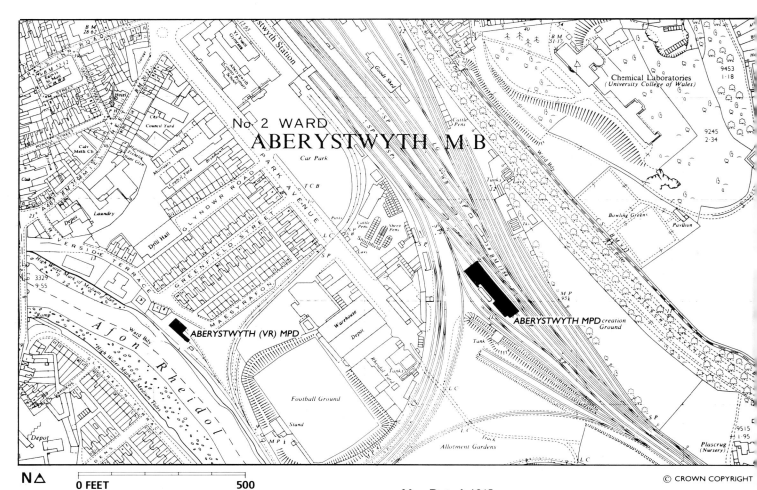

Upon closure of the standard gauge shed, the depot was converted to narrow gauge and the locomotives were transferred from the original VR shed in the same year.

Map Dated: 1965

Site Location: Aberystwyth Station is located in the south east of the town.

Track Status: Aberystwyth Station and lines are operational.

87H(s) CARDIGAN

Location: North of the line, adjacent to Cardigan Station. (OS Map Ref: SN181458)

Directions: Entrance to the shed is effected from the station platform.

Closed: September 1962.

Description: A brick built 1TS through road shed.

Post Closure History: *Demolished. Site is now occupied by a motor vehicle repair garage. (1989)*

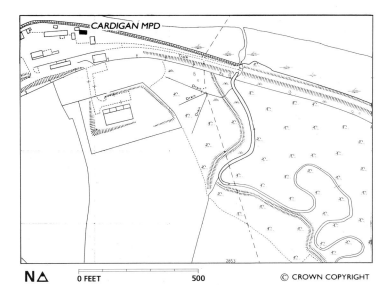

N△ 0 FEET 500 © CROWN COPYRIGHT

Map Dated: 1975 (Shed Superimposed)

Site Location: In the south of the town, east of Tenby Road (A478) and on the south bank of the River Teifi.

Track Status: Cardigan Station closed in 1962. Lines lifted.

CARDIGAN MPD at the point of closure, and not a moment too soon from its dilapidated appearance on September 19th, 1962. *WT Stubbs Collection*

Photograph Courtesy of BBC In The Midlands

GARDENING CORNER

The site of one of British Railways Motive Power Depots found unexpected fame during 1988.

BBC In The Midlands were looking for a new housing estate with undeveloped gardens to use in a programme called *"First Time Gardening"* and co-incidentally a local firm had just sold off their Transport Depot for re-development as one.

Those intrepid gardeners *Geoff Hamilton* and *Gay Search* were despatched to the site and a new garden was duly produced over a number of programmes which were transmitted during October of that year.

The local firm was Cadbury-Schweppes and those of us blighted with greenfly rather than blessed with green fingers can only admire the transformation of **BOURNVILLE MPD** shed yard, the occupant of the site before the building of the Transport Depot, into a beautiful garden.

CARMARTHENSHIRE

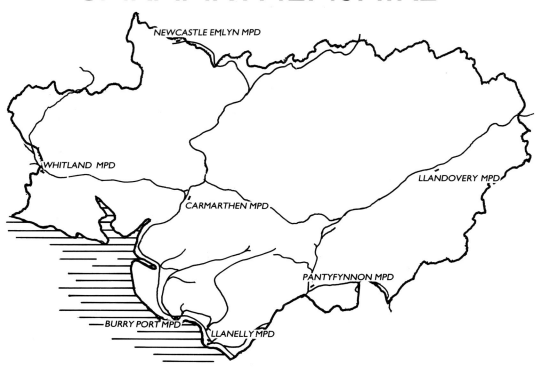

NEWCASTLE EMLYN MPD

WHITLAND MPD

LLANDOVERY MPD

CARMARTHEN MPD

PANTYFYNNON MPD

BURRY PORT MPD

LLANELLY MPD

87F LLANELLY

Location: Adjacent to Llanelly Dockland. (OS Map Ref: SS514855)

Directions: Turn right outside of Llanelly Station, right over the level crossing into New Dock Road, left into Dolau Road, pass under the railway bridges into Embankment Road and the shed entrance is a gate on the left hand side just past the last of these bridges.

Closed: September 14th, 1965.

Description: A brick built double roundhouse shed.

Post Closure History: Demolished. The entire site is now grazing land for horses. (1989)

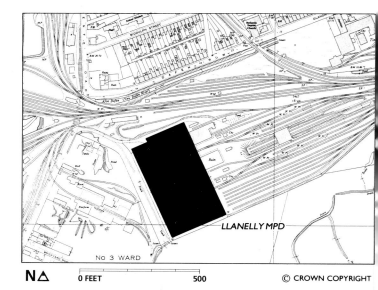

LLANELLY MPD

NO 3 WARD

N△   0 FEET   500   © CROWN COPYRIGHT

Map Dated: 1952

Site Location: In the south of the town, just south east of Great Western Dock.

Track Status: Lines lifted.

Horses now graze where this massive shed building once stood. **LLANELLY MPD** was photographed on September 21st, 1962.
WT Stubbs Collection

87F(s) BURRY PORT

Location: In Burry Dockland. (OS Map Ref: SN447006)

Directions: Leave Pembrey & Burry Port Station by the southern exit. Go ahead past the rear of Burry Port (BPGVR) Station and bear round to the left. The shed entrance is on the right hand side.

Closed: February 24th, 1962.

Description: A wooden built 3TS shed with 2 through roads.

Post Closure History: *Demolished with floors traceable. Site unused, in a patch of wasteland. (1989)*

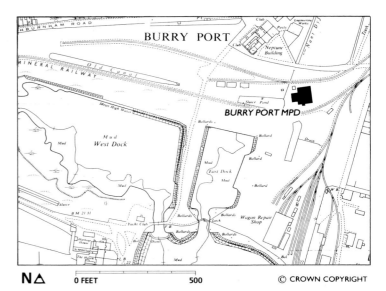

NΔ   0 FEET   500   © CROWN COPYRIGHT

Map Dated: 1969

Site Location: In the south of the town, south of the B4361.

Track Status: Pembrey & Burry Port Station and line are operational.

BURRY PORT MPD shortly after closure on September 21st, 1962.
WT Stubbs Collection

87F(s) PANTYFYNNON

Location: West of the Ammanford line, north of Pantyfynnon Station. (OS Map Ref: SN625112)

Directions: Turn right over the level crossing, at the north end of the station, bear left almost immediately and a cinder path on the right hand side leads to the shed.

Closed: August 1964.

Description: A corrugated iron 4TS through road shed.

Post Closure History: *Demolished with floors traceable. The coaling stage ramp and two tracks are still in situ in the shed yard. Site Unused.*

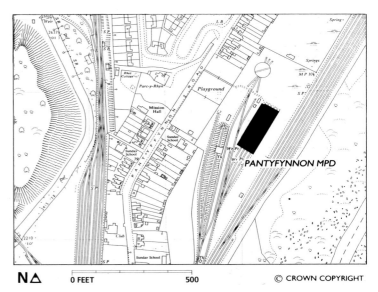

NΔ   0 FEET   500   © CROWN COPYRIGHT

Map Dated: 1962

Site Location: South of Ammanford, on the east side of the A483.

Track Status: Pantyfynnon Station and line are operational.

PANTYFFYNON MPD nearing the end of its operational life, photographed on September 21st, 1962   *WT Stubbs Collection*

87G CARMARTHEN

Location: On the east side of the line, south of Carmarthen Station, and adjacent to Carmarthen Junction Station. (OS Map Ref: SN413196)

Directions: Turn right outside Carmarthen Station along the approach road, right over the railway bridge and fork right at the end of this bridge. A cinder path leads to the shed from the right hand side of this road.

Closed: April 13th, 1964.

Description: A brick built 8TS dead ended shed.

Post Closure History: Demolished with floors traceable. Site unused. (1989)

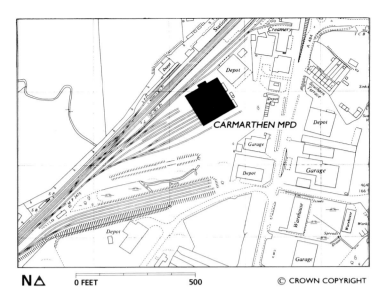

N△   0 FEET   500   © CROWN COPYRIGHT

Map Dated: 1969 (Shed Superimposed)
Site Location: South of the town centre, west of the A484.
Track Status: Carmarthen Station and line are operational.

The spacious layout of **CARMARTHEN MPD**, is evident in this view photographed on September 20th, 1962.   *WT Stubbs Collection*

87G(s) NEWCASTLE EMLYN

Location: North of the line, at the east end of Newcastle Emlyn Station. (OS Map Ref: SN315405)

Directions: Entrance to the shed is effected from the station platform.

Closed: September 15th, 1952.

Description: A corrugated iron 1TS through road shed.

Post Closure History: Demolished. The shed site is now part of rear garden to Pandy Mill.

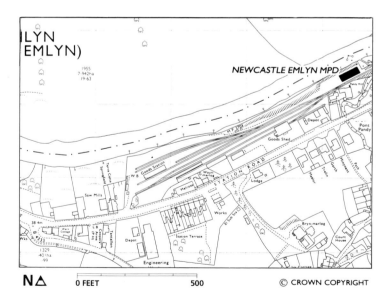

N△   0 FEET   500   © CROWN COPYRIGHT

Map Dated: 1974 (Shed Superimposed)
Site Location: West of the town centre, on the south bank of the River Teifi
Track Status: Newcastle Emlyn Station closed in 1952. Lines lifted.

The rudimentary shed building, complete with cut-out to accomodate the locomotive's chimney, at **NEWCASTLE EMLYN MPD**.   *Bernard Matthews Collection*

87H(s) WHITLAND

Location: South side of Whitland Station. (OS Map Ref: SN199164)
Directions: Turn right outside of the station, cross the level crossing and turn right into the Goods Yard. A pathway in this yard leads to the shed.
Closed: September 9th, 1963.
Description: A corrugated iron 1TS through road shed.
Post Closure History: *Demolished. A caravan sales business occupies the shed site. (1989)*

Ex-GWR 4500 Class 2–6–2T No. 5520 straddles the ash pit on the shed road at **WHITLAND MPD**. *Bernard Matthews Collection*

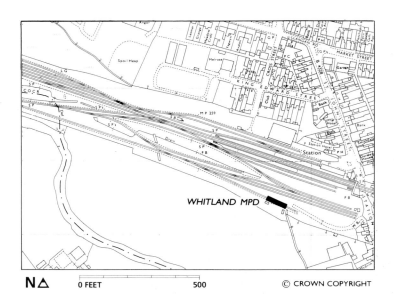

N△   0 FEET   500   © CROWN COPYRIGHT

Map Dated: 1970 (Shed Superimposed)
Site Location: West of the town, on the west side of St. John's Street (B4328)
Track Status: Whitland Station and line are operational.

87K(s) LLANDOVERY

Location: East of the line, south of Llandovery Station. OS Map Ref: SN761343)
Directions: Entrance to the shed is effected from the Goods Yard, adjacent to the Station entrance.
Closed: August 10th, 1964.
Description: A brick built 4TS dead ended shed
Post Closure History: *Demolished with floors traceable. Site now used for coal storage. (1989)*

The former LNWR outpost at **LLANDOVERY MPD** was looking decidedly shabby when photographed on August 8th, 1954. *WT Stubbs Collection*

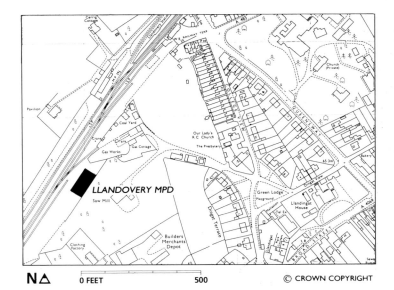

N△   0 FEET   500   © CROWN COPYRIGHT

Map Dated: 1978 (Shed Superimposed)
Site Location: West of the town centre, on the west side of Queensway (A40)
Track Status: Llandovery Station and line are operational.

MONTGOMERYSHIRE

89A(s) WELSHPOOL (W&LLR)
Location: South of the Llanfair line between Seven Stars and Welshpool Stations. (OS Map Ref: SJ229074)
Directions: Turn right outside of Welshpool Station along the lane and upon reaching the level crossing turn left and follow the narrow gauge track. This leads to the shed.
Closed: November 5th, 1956. (Line Closure Date)
Description: A corrugated iron 1TS dead ended shed. (The gauge of the lines is 2ft 6ins)
***Post Closure History**: Demolished*

Ex-WLLR 0–6–0T No. 823 receives attention and a full tank of water outside the small corrugated iron shed at **WELSHPOOL (W&LLR) MPD** on June 26th, 1951.
Allan Sommerfield Collection

Welshpool & Llanfair Light Railway is now owned and operated by a pre-servation group, but the line has not been re-instated in the east part of the town.

89A(s) WELSHPOOL
Location: East of the line, north of Welshpool Station. (OS Map Ref: SJ231074)
Directions: Entrance to the shed is effected from the station platform.
Out of Use: 1954
Description: Originally a 2TS through road shed, demolished in the 1930s, by BR days it consisted of 2 stand sidings and Engine Pits. There are no shed buildings.
***Post Closure History**: Lines lifted*

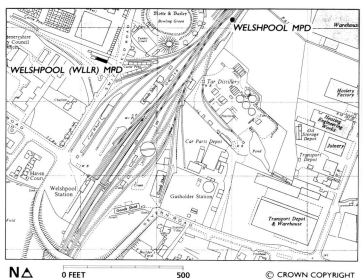

Map Dated: 1967 (Welshpool W&LLR Shed Superimposed)
Site Location: South east of the town centre, at the end of Severn Road.
Track Status: Welshpool Station and line are operational, W&LLR lines lifted.

89A(s) LLANFYLLIN

Location: South of the line, east of Llanfyllin Station. (OS Map Ref: SJ148192)
Directions: A path from the station yard leads to the shed.
Closed: September 27th 1952.
Description: A corrugated iron 1TS dead ended shed.
Post Closure History: Demolished

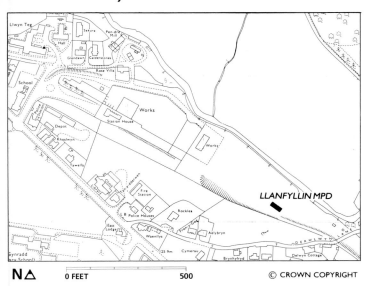

N△   0 FEET   500   © CROWN COPYRIGHT

Map Dated: 1975 (Shed Superimposed)
Site Location: In the east of the town, on the south bank of the River Cain.
Track Status: Llanfyllin Station closed in 1965. Lines lifted.

89A(s) LLANIDLOES

Location: East of the line, at the north end of Llanidloes Station. (OS Map Ref: SN958845)
Directions: Entrance to the shed is effected from the station platform.
Closed: December 31st, 1962.
Description: A brick built 2TS dead ended shed.
Post Closure History: Demolished. Shed floor traceable. (1987)

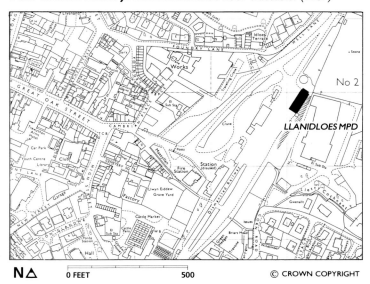

N△   0 FEET   500   © CROWN COPYRIGHT

Map Dated: 1981
Site Location: In the east of the town, east of Cambrian Place.
Track Status: Llanidloes Station closed in 1962. Lines lifted

89C MACHYNLLETH

Location: South of the line, east of Machynlleth Station. (OS Map Ref: SH747015)
Directions: A drive leads from the east end of the station approach to the shed.
Closed: December 5th, 1966 (Steam)
Description: A stone built 3TS shed with two through roads.
Post Closure History: Still Standing. In use as a Diesel Depot (Code MN). (1988)

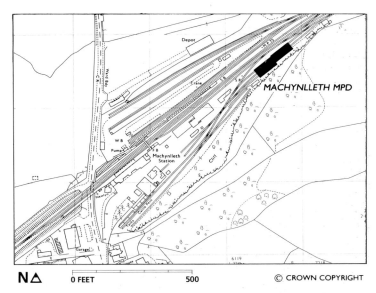

N△   0 FEET   500   © CROWN COPYRIGHT

Map Dated: 1974
Site Location: In the north of the town, on the east side of the A487.
Track Status: Machynlleth Station and line are operational.

*BR Class 2 2–6–0 No. 78003 stands at the station end of **MACHYNLLETH MPD** on July 28th, 1961.*
Ken Fairey

89A(s) MOAT LANE

Location: In the fork of the Machynlleth and Brecon lines, adjacent to Moat Lane Junction Station. (OS Map Ref: SO043991)

Directions: Entrance to the shed is gained from the footpath at the west end of the station.

Closed: December 31st, 1962.

Description: A wooden built 2TS dead ended shed.

Post Closure History: *Still Standing. In use as a Barn (1988)*

The relatively remotely sited **MOAT LANE MPD** on August 10th, 1958 some years before assuming its current role as a barn.   *Alec Swain*

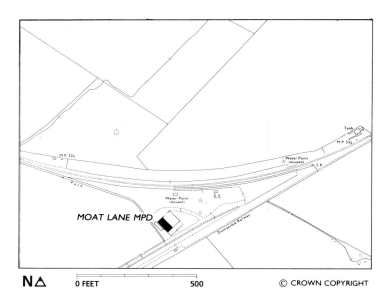

Map Dated: 1974

Site Location: About 1 mile south east of Caersws, at the end of a pathway running south east from the A492 and running parallel to the line.

Track Status: Moat Lane Junction Station closed in 1962. The Machynlleth line is operational, the Brecon line is lifted.

89A(s) KERRY

Location: West of the line, north of Kerry Station. (OS Map Ref: SO164904)

Directions: Entrance to the shed is effected from the station platform.

Closed: February 9th, 1931, subsequently used as a Stabling Point.

Description: A corrugated iron 1TS dead-ended shed.

Post Closure History: *Still Standing. In use as a barn (1987)*

KERRY MPD, was 'home' for a caravan when photographed on May 21st, 1961.   *WT Stubbs Collection*

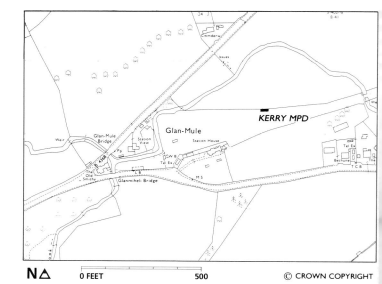

Map Dated: 1975

Site Location: At Glanmule in the fork of the A489 and B4368 roads, about one mile east of Kerry.

Track Status: Kerry Station closed in 1931. Lines lifted.

MERIONETHSHIRE

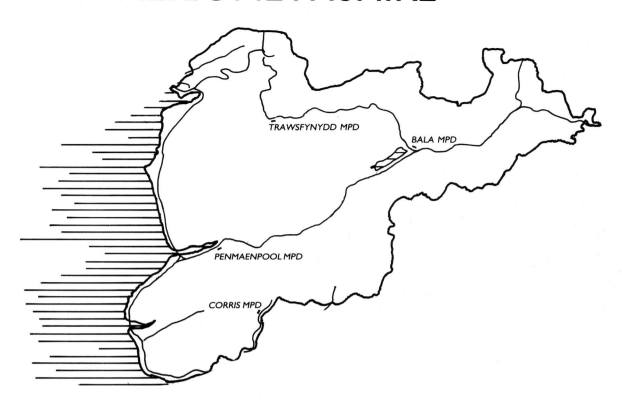

TRAWSFYNYDD MPD

BALA MPD

PENMAENPOOL MPD

CORRIS MPD

84J(s) BALA
Location: North of the line, east of Bala Station. (OS Map Ref: SH931359)
Directions: Entrance to the shed is effected from the station platform.
Closed: January 18th, 1965.
Description: A brick built ITS dead ended shed.
Post Closure History: Demolished. Site of Industrial development. (1989)

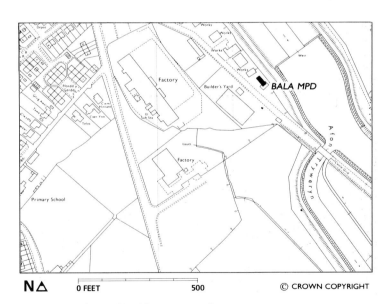

N△   0 FEET   500   © CROWN COPYRIGHT

Map Dated: 1978 (Shed Superimposed)
Site Location: In the south east of the town, on the west bank of the Afon Tryweryn.
Track Status: Bala Station closed in 1965. Lines lifted.

BALA MPD typically houses a couple of 0–6–0PT locomotives on August 10th, 1958.
Alec Swain

84J(s) PENMAENPOOL

Location: South of the line, west of Penmaenpool Station. (OS Map Ref: SH692184)

Directions: On leaving the station turn right along the A493 (to Towyn) and a footpath about 300 yards on the right hand side leads to the shed.

Closed: January 18th, 1965

Description: A wooden built 2TS dead ended shed.

Post Closure History: Still standing, with lines lifted as late as 1975, but subsequently demolished. Site Unused.

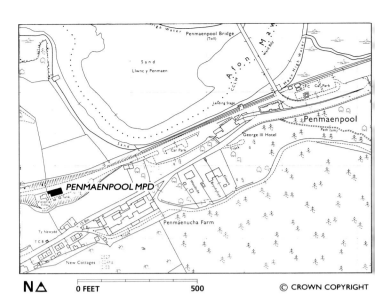

Map Dated: 1982 (Shed Superimposed)
Site Location: On the north side of the A493, on the south bank of the River Mawddach.
Track Status: Penmaenpool Station closed in 1965. Lines lifted.

A typical scene at **PENMAENPOOL MPD** on September 11th, 1960
WT Stubbs Collection

84J(s) TRAWSFYNYDD

Location: South of the line, at the east end of Trawsfynydd Station. (OS Map Ref: SH715360)

Directions: Entrance to the shed is effected from the station platform.

Closed: January 1961.

Description: A brick built 1TS through road shed, in the form of a lean-to adjoining the Goods Shed.

Post Closure History: Still Standing. In agricultural use. (1989)

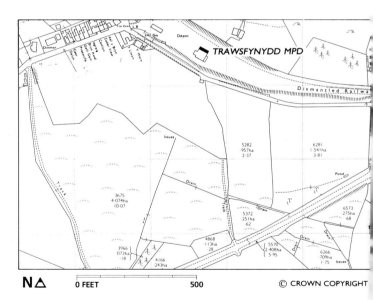

Map Dated: 1975
Site Location: On the east side of the A470, north of the town.
Track Status: Trawsfynydd Station closed in 1960. Lines lifted.

An 0–6–0PT occupies what must be one of the most economically built sheds on BR. **TRAWSFYNYDD MPD** was merely an additional brick wall and slated roof attached to the side of the Goods Shed and was photographed on September 11th, 1960. *WT Stubbs Collection*

39C(s) CORRIS

Location: In the fork of the Machynlleth to Upper Corris and Corris lines, south of Corris Station. (OS Map Ref: SH753068)
Directions: The entrance to the shed is adjacent to the A487 on the east side of the road, about 800 yards south of Corris.
Closed: July 31st, 1948 (Line Closure Date)
Description: A stone built 1TS dead ended shed
Post Closure History: *Still Standing.(1989)*

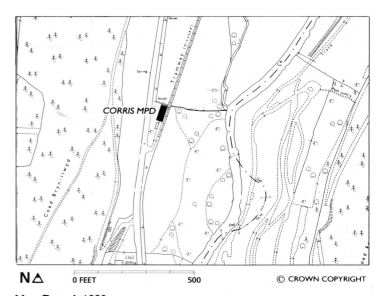

Fourteen years on from closure and **CORRIS MPD** still looked in fine shape. The former Corris Railway depot was in private use when viewed on September 19th, 1962.   *WT Stubbs Collection*

NA   0 FEET   500   © CROWN COPYRIGHT

Map Dated: 1980
Track Status: Corris Station closed in 1931. Lines lifted.
The shed has been taken over by a preservation group and the track is in the process of being relaid.

MERTHYR MPD plays host to ex-LNWR Coal Tank 0–6–2T No. 58926 on *Stephenson Locomotive Society* duty on January 5th, 1958.   *Sid Nash*

RADNORSHIRE

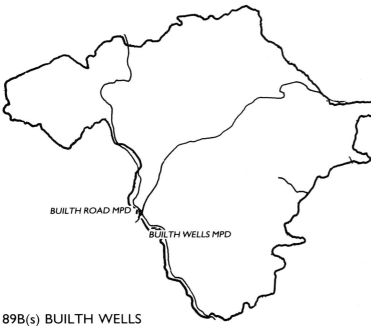

84G(s) BUILTH ROAD

Location: West of the line, south of Builth Road Station. (OS Map Re
SO024528)
Directions: Entrance to the shed is effected from the station platform.
Closed: December 31st, 1962.
Description: A wooden built 1TS dead ended shed.
*Post Closure History: Demolished. The entire site and connecting curv
is now part of a large timber yard for Economic Forestry Group PLC. Th
shed floor is traceable and partially buried under wood shavings. (1989)*

The small wooden shed at **BUILTH ROAD MPD** on May 21st, 1961.
WT Stubbs Collectior

89B(s) BUILTH WELLS

Location: South of the line, east of Builth Wells Station. (OS Map Ref:
SO043515)
Directions: Entrance to the shed is effected from the station platform.
Closed: September 14th, 1957.
Description: A corrugated iron 1TS dead ended shed.
*Post Closure History: Demolished. The shed site is part of a grassed car
park for the adjacent County Showground. (1989)*

BUILTH WELLS MPD still looks in good condition despite being officially closed
for over three years. Photographed on May 21st, 1961. *WT Stubbs Collection*

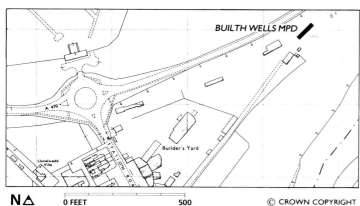

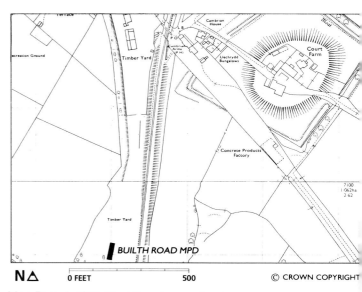

Map Dated: 1973 (Shed Superimposed)
Site Location: About 2 miles north west of Builth Wells, on the wes
side of the A470
Track Status: Builth Road (High Level) Station and line are operationa
Builth Road (Low Level) Station closed in 1962. Lines lifted.

◀ **Map Dated**: 1974 (Shed Superimposed)
Site Location: On the north side of the town, east of Station Road.
Track Status: Builth Wells Station closed in 1962. Lines lifted.

PEMBROKESHIRE

FISHGUARD (GOODWICK) MPD

MILFORD HAVEN MPD

NEYLAND MPD

PEMBROKE DOCK MPD

87H NEYLAND

Location: Situated between the lines, north of Neyland Station. (OS Map Ref: SM967051)

Directions: Entrance to the shed is effected from the station yard.

Closed: September 9th, 1963.

Description: A wooden built 2TS shed with 1 through road.

Post Closure History: *Demolished. Entire site is now occupied by a Marina. (1989)*

A general view of the shed yard and facilities at **NEYLAND MPD** on September 20th, 1962.
WT Stubbs Collection

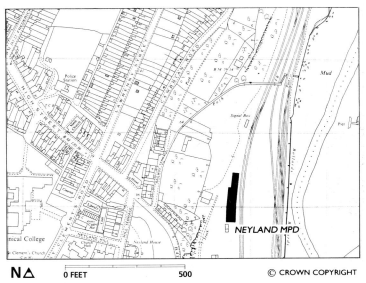

NEYLAND MPD

N△   0 FEET   500   © CROWN COPYRIGHT

Map Dated: 1968 (Shed Superimposed)

Site Location: South east of the town centre, east of the High Street (B4324)

Track Status: Neyland Station closed in 1964. Lines lifted.
Some track, although severed, remains in situ in the quayside.

87H(s) MILFORD HAVEN

Location: East of the line, north of Milford Haven Station. (OS Map Ref: SM901064)

Directions: Entrance to the shed is effected from the station platform.

Closed: December 1962.

Description: A brick built 1TS dead ended shed.

Post Closure History: *Demolished with floors traceable. Site Unused.* (1989)

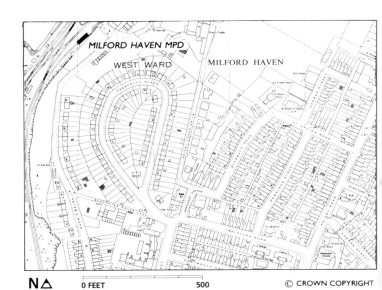

Map Dated: 1970 (Shed Superimposed)
Site Location: In the west of the town.
Track Status: Milford Haven Station and line are operational.

The small shed building at **MILFORD HAVEN MPD** on September 20th, 1962.
WT Stubbs Collection

87H(s) PEMBROKE DOCK

Location: West of the line, south of Pembroke Dock Station. (OS Map Ref:)

Directions: Entrance to the shed is effected from the station platform.

Closed: September 9th, 1963.

Description: A stone built 2TS dead ended shed with corrugated iron extension.

Post Closure History: *Demolished, with part of one wall still standing. Floor traceable. Site Unused.*

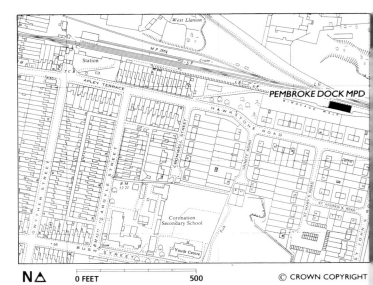

Map Dated: 1968 (Shed Superimposed)
Site Location: In the centre of the town.
Track Status: Pembroke Dock Station and line are operational.

A quiet interlude at **PEMBROKE DOCK MPD** on September 20th, 1962.
WT Stubbs Collection

87J FISHGUARD GOODWICK

Location: On the west side of the line, south of Fishguard & Goodwick station. (OS Map Ref: SM944380)

Directions: Turn sharp left outside the station over the railway bridge, turn left at the end and fork left parallel to the railway. A flight of steps leads to the shed from a gate on the left hand side.

Closed: September 9th, 1963

Description: A brick built 2TS dead ended shed.

Post Closure History: Demolished. Now site of Goodwick Industrial Estate. (1989)

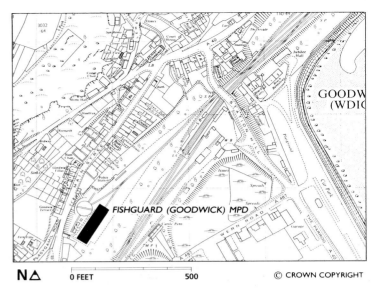

N△   0 FEET   500   © CROWN COPYRIGHT

Map Dated: 1965

Site Location: North West of Fishguard, on the north side of Wern Road (A487).

Track Status: Fishguard & Goodwick Station closed in 1964. Line operational.

A fine view of all the facilities at **FISHGUARD GOODWICK MPD** taken on September 20th, 1962.
WT Stubbs Collection

SALTLEY MPD was certainly in the throes of rebuilding when this view of ex-MR Class 2F 0–6–0 No. 58230 was taken on October 9th, 1955. The refurbishment of the depot was not finally completed until the late 1950s, a typical piece of capital investment undertaken during that period to see steam through to its projected end, only to be overtaken by the speed of events and prove to be of little value at great cost. The depot closed less than ten years later and was demolished with barely a few fragments remaining.
Ken Fairey

BRECKNOCK

89B BRECON

Location: On the south side of the line, east of Brecon Station. (OS Map Ref SO053281)

Directions: Turn left outside the station along the approach road, continue into Camden Road, turn left into Free Street, left into Watton and left again into the Goods Yard Approach Road. This road leads to the shed.

Closed: December 31st, 1962. *(Regarded as a Stabling Point only from November 2nd, 1959)*

Description: A brick built 2TS through road shed.

Post Closure History: *Demolished. Now site of car park for Welsh Water office block. (1989)*

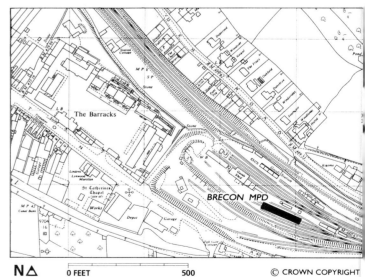

Map Dated: 1964
Site Location: In the south east of the town, on the north side of the A40
Track Status: Brecon Station closed in 1962. Lines lifted.

Ex-LMS 2–6–0 No. 46520 stands outside **BRECON MPD** on April 20th 1958.
Ken Fairey

87K(s) GURNOS

Location: In the fork of the Brynamman and Yniscedwyn Colliery lines, north of Ystalyfera Station. (OS Map Ref: SN774095)

Directions: The shed entrance is a gate on the left hand side of the A4068 main Ystalyfera to Brynamman road, just past the bridge over the mineral line to Yniscedwyn Colliery.

Closed: April 2nd, 1962.

Description: A brick built 2TS dead ended shed.

Post Closure History: *Demolished. A grass verge now occupies the shed site and the Yniscedwyn Colliery line is buried under the A4067.*

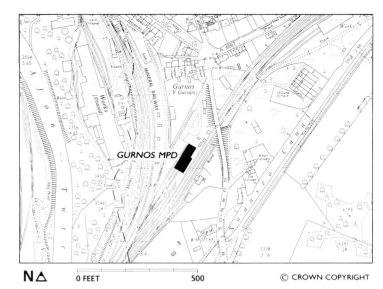

N△   0 FEET   500   © CROWN COPYRIGHT

Map Dated: 1964

Site Location: In the south of the town, adjacent to the west side of Gurnos Road (A4068) and the north bank of the Swansea Canal.

Track Status: Lines lifted.

One of the few ex-LMS sheds that penetrated into deepest South Wales, **GURNOS MPD** in pre-BR times.   *Bernard Matthews Collection*

The adoption of former railway routes, particularly in rural areas, as roadways and bypasses has, since the 1960s at least been successfully achieved by Road Traffic Engineers. It is difficult to believe, in this view of **GURNOS MPD**, that anything other than roads ever occupied the site which at one time was a busy railway centre.
The roadway in the middle distance is built on the colliery line trackbed, which the road in the foreground originally bridged but has now been excavated to link up with the new road. The shed site was on the right hand side of the picture.

Paul Smith

PART NINE
NORTH WALES

DENBIGH ANGLESEY FLINT CARNARVONSHIRE

HOLYHEAD

ANGLESEY

BANGOR

CARNARVONSHIRE

RHYL

FLINT

DENBIGH

DENBIGH

BRITISH RAILWAYS

PORTMADOC MPD *(John Edgington)*

DENBIGH

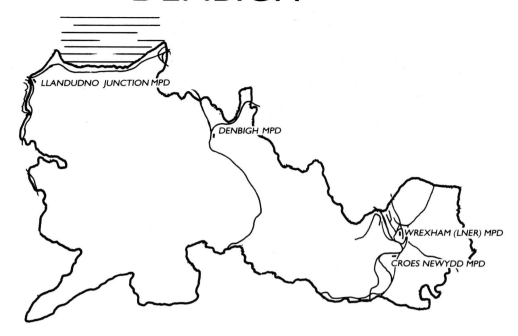

LLANDUDNO JUNCTION MPD

DENBIGH MPD

WREXHAM (LNER) MPD

CROES NEWYDD MPD

SE WREXHAM (LNER)

Location: West of the line, north of Wrexham Exchange Station. (OS Map Ref: SJ330516)

Directions: Turn right outside of the main entrance to Wrexham General Station and turn right along Mold Road, crossing the railway. Turn first right along Crispin Lane and a broad path leads up a short bank to the shed opposite the end of this road.

Closed: January 4th, 1960

Description: A brick built 6TS dead ended shed.

Post Closure History: Demolished.

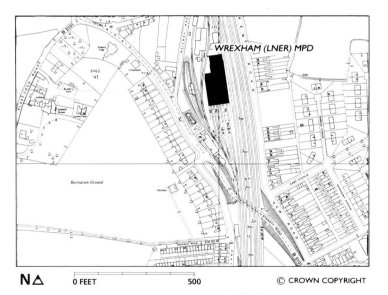

WREXHAM (LNER) MPD

NΔ   0 FEET — 500   © CROWN COPYRIGHT

Map Dated: 1960.

Site Location: North west of the town centre, on the east side of Stansty Road (B5101)

Track Status: Wrexham Exchange Station closed in 1982. Line operational.

Tank engines of various origins and vintage line up outside of **WREXHAM (LNER) MPD** on April 5th, 1959.
Ken Fairey

7A LLANDUDNO JUNCTION

Location: On a goods loop, south of Llandudno Junction Station. (OS Map Ref: SH795775)

Directions: Turn right outside of the station into Conway Road, and then right into Queens Road, continue over the bridge over the line and a footpath immediately on the right leads to the shed.

Closed: October 3rd, 1966.

Description: A brick built 4TS through road shed.

Post Closure History: The shed buildings have been demolished, and a rudimentary diesel depot (Code LJ) has been established in the carriage shed, alongside the shed site.(1987)

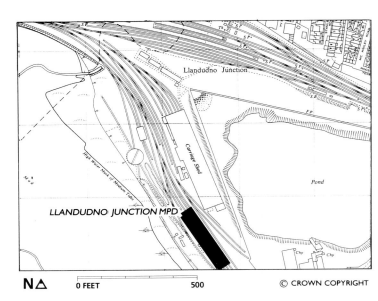

N△   0 FEET   500   © CROWN COPYRIGHT

Map Dated: 1960
Site Location: South of the A55, on the east bank of the River Conway.
Track Status: Llandudno Junction and line are operational

LLANDUDNO JUNCTION MPD plays host to a fine collection of ex-LMS engines on June 5th, 1960.   *Ken Fairey*

7D(s) DENBIGH

Location: East of the line, north of Denbigh Station. (OS Map Ref: SJ059671)

Directions: Turn left outside of Denbigh Station, left again and proceed under the railway bridge. Turn first left along Rhyl Road and after about half a mile turn left again. The shed entrance is on the left hand side, just before the level crossing.

Closed: September 19th, 1955.

Description: A brick built 2TS dead ended shed

Post Closure History: Still Standing (1987).

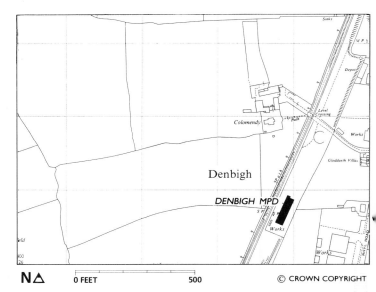

N△   0 FEET   500   © CROWN COPYRIGHT

Map Dated: 1967
Site Location: In the north of the town, on the west side of the A525.
Track Status: Denbigh Station closed in 1962. Lines lifted.

DENBIGH MPD on September 14th, 1952.   *John Edgington*

84J CROES NEWYDD

Location: In the triangle formed by the Ruabon to Wrexham to Brymbo lines. (OS Map Ref: SJ327501)
Directions: Leave Wrexham General Station by the main exit and turn left into Regent Street, right into Bradley Road and right into Watery Road. A path leads to the shed from a gate on the left hand side, just past the level crossing.
Closed: June 5th, 1967.
Description: A brick built roundhouse.
Post Closure History: Demolished.

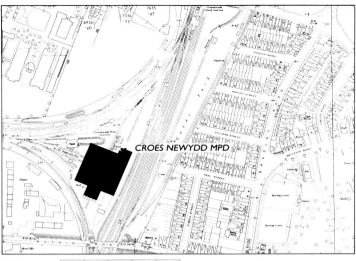

NΔ 0 FEET 500 © CROWN COPYRIGHT

Map Dated: 1960
Site Location: In the west of Wrexham on the west side of Bradley Road (B5100)
Track Status: Wrexham General Station and lines are operational.

Ex-LMS Class 5 4–6–0 No. 45198, looking relatively clean and tidy, stands in the shed yard at **CROES NEWYDD MPD** on August 19th, 1966   *Ken Fairey*

PWLLYRHEBOG *(Bill Potter)*

ANGLESEY

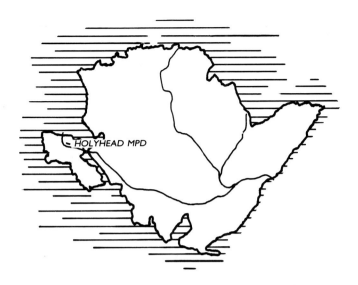

7A HOLYHEAD

Location: East of the line, south of Holyhead Station. (OS Map Ref: SH249818)

Directions: Leave the station by the main drive, turn left into London Road and right into Wheston Street. The shed entrance is at the end of this street.

Closed: December 5th, 1966 (Steam)

Description: A brick built 4TS dead ended shed.

Post Closure History: Still Standing. In use as a diesel depot (Code HD) (1989).

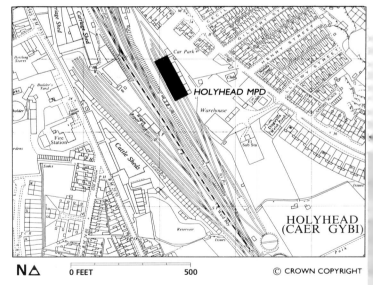

Map Dated: 1968
Site Location: In the south of the town, on the west side of the A5.
Track Status: Holyhead Station and line are operational.

One of BRs outposts, **HOLYHEAD MPD** found fame servicing, as well as having some allocated, many of the ex-LMS main line passenger engines engaged in Boat Train Expresses. This view shows a Royal Scot Class 4–6–0 amongst a cluster of sundry freight locomotives.   *Bernard Matthews Collection*

FLINT

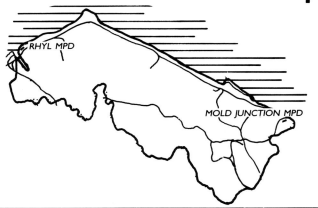

7D RHYL

Location: North of the line, west of Rhyl Station. (OS Map Ref: SJ006810)
Directions: Go straight ahead out of the station into Bodfor Street, turn left into Kinmel Street, left into Elwy Street, right into West Kinmel Street and left into Ffynnongroew Road. The shed entrance is on the left hand side.
Closed: February 11th, 1963.
Description: A brick built 3TS dead ended shed.
Post Closure History: Demolished. The site is now a Car Park. (1989)

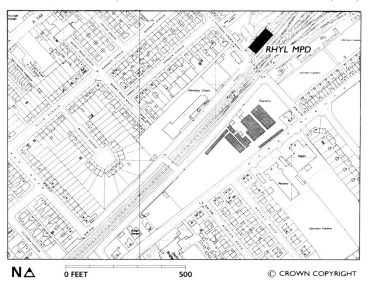

N△   0 FEET   500   © CROWN COPYRIGHT

Map Dated: 1961
Site Location: South of the town, west of Vale Road Bridge (A525)
Track Status: Rhyl Station and line are operational.

Ex-LMS engines line up outside of **RHYL MPD** on September 14th, 1952.
John Edgington

6B MOLD JUNCTION

Location: South of the Chester to North Wales line, about 3.5 miles west of Chester. (OS Map Ref: SJ368651)
Directions: The shed entrance is on the west side of the B5129, Saltney to Queensferry Road, just south of the point where it crosses the North Wales line.
Closed: April 18th, 1966.
Description: A brick built 8TS dead ended shed.
Post Closure History: Still Standing, in derelict condition. (1988)

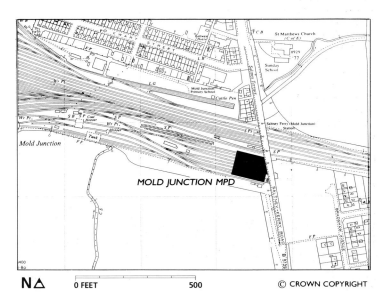

N△   0 FEET   500   © CROWN COPYRIGHT

Map Dated: 1961
Track Status: Line operational

A typically mixed bag of locomotives assemble outside of **MOLD JUNCTION MPD** on May 1st, 1960.
WT Stubbs

CARNARVONSHIRE

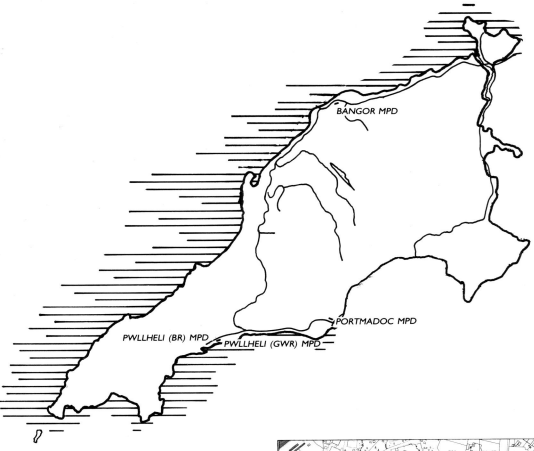

7B BANGOR
Location: On the south side of the line, adjacent to Bangor Station. (OS Map Ref: SH575716)

Directions: Turn right out of the station yard, proceed down the hill and turn right at the bottom under the railway bridge. The shed entrance is a door in the wall on the right hand side, just past the bridge.

Closed: June 14th, 1965.

Description: A brick built 6TS dead ended shed.

Post Closure History: Still Standing. In commercial use. (1987)

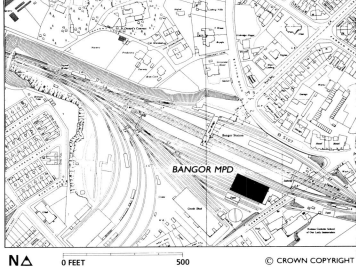

Map Dated: 1967

Site Location: In the centre of the town, on the south side of Station Road (B5107)

Track Status: Bangor Station and line are operational.

A busy scene at **BANGOR MPD** on May 28th, 1961.   *WT Stubbs Collection*

89C(s) PWLLHELI (BR)

Location: South of the line, east of Pwllheli Station. (OS Map Ref: SH383352)

Directions: Turn left outside of the station into Station Square and immediately left along a road. Continue along a rough road between the harbour and the line and turn right at the end into the Goods Yard. The shed is in this yard.

Closed: 1966

Description: A brick built 2TS dead ended shed

Post Closure History: *Still Standing. (1989)*

The new shed, **PWLLHELI BR MPD**, photographed on July 15th, 1959, was built on a different site in the Goods Yard with considerably more spacious and convenient accomodation for the locomotives.
Sid Nash

89C(s) PWLLHELI (GWR)

Location: South of the line, east of Pwllheli Station. (OS Map Ref: SH382353)

Directions: For directions see under PWLLHELI (BR) SHED.

Out of Use: 1959 (Locomotives moved to new BR-built shed)

Description: A corrugated iron 1TS dead ended shed.

Post Closure History: *Demolished*

The unusual length of **PWLLHELI GWR MPD** is captured in this 1949 view of the shed.
Allan Sommerfield Collection

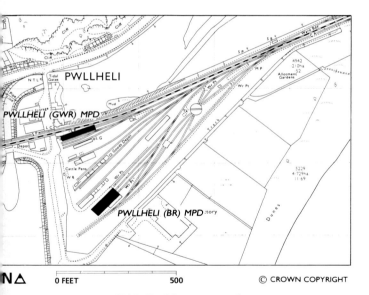

Map Dated: 1970 (Ex-GWR Shed Superimposed)

Site Location: East of the town, south of the A497.

Track Status: Pwllheli Station and line are operational.

89C(s) PORTMADOC

Location: North of the line, at the west end of Portmadoc Station. (OS Map Ref: SH565392)

Directions: Entrance to the shed is effected from the station platform.

Closed: August 1963.

Description: A brick built 2TS dead ended shed.

Post Closure History: *Demolished, Site Unused (1975)*

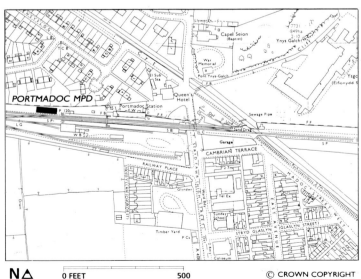

Map Dated: 1970 (Shed Superimposed)

Site Location: North of the town, on the west side of the A487.

Track Status: Portmadoc Station and line are operational.

INDEX